Forth Application Techniques
Course Notebook

FORTH, Inc.

FORTH, Inc.
Los Angeles, California
www.forth.com

Contents

Section 7: Vectored Execution

Section 8: Advanced Concepts

Section 9: File Operations

Section 10: Multitasking

Section 11: Style Recommendations

About This Book

This book was designed to support classes in Forth programming taught at FORTH, Inc. My colleagues and I at FORTH, Inc. have been training Forth programmers since 1973, and literally thousands of programmers from all over the world have taken our courses.

Some of the material in this book, therefore, found its way into our training curriculum years ago. Other sections are new; reflecting not only changes in Forth systems and usage, but also new ways to present challenging material, such as defining words (Section 8.6). I have written some parts, and others have been written by some of the excellent instructors I've worked with over the years. Among these are Kim Harris, Al Krever, Randy Leberknight, Ned Conklin, and Gary Sprung. I'm grateful to all of them.

The course is intended to introduce Forth to people with little or no prior experience in the language. However, it does assume the reader is familiar with general computing concepts (bytes, memory, addresses, data objects, etc.). Prior programming experience in some language is helpful, though not required.

There are three major components of a course:

1. Lectures
2. Supporting text with examples
3. Problems for the student to solve

If you are not using this book in a class, the first element is missing. Realistically, this means you'll miss a lot of background details and explanations of why things work the way they do. In that case, we strongly recommend that you supplement this book with a more detailed text on Forth, such as *Forth Programmer's Handbook* (available at www.forth.com).

However, of these three elements, the most important is student problem solving. No lectures or text can do more than provide a context for working the problems, which is where the real learning takes place. We urge you, therefore, to work all the problems in this book on a Forth system. Although we've used FORTH, Inc. products for our classes and some clearly marked, product-specific functions are discussed in this book, virtually all the problems can be worked on any Standard Forth system. Use a programmer's editor to edit your work in files, and load them following instructions for the system you're using.

When you work problems, always strive for the shortest and simplest solution. No problem in this book requires more than a few lines of code. Also, try to follow the style guidelines in Section 11. The most important stylistic element, which we require of all our students, is to start each definition with a stack comment (discussed in Section 2.2.2 and Section 11.1.1). By doing this you'll help yourself visualize how your definition should work as you write it.

By following these guidelines you can become not only a Forth programmer, but a good Forth programmer.

Solutions to the problems in this book are available on our web site:

www.forth.com/answers

Good luck!

Elizabeth D. Rather
FORTH, Inc.

Section 1: Introduction

1.1 A Brief History of Forth

The Forth programming language was originally developed by Charles H. Moore. Although it evolved over a number of years, the first true standalone Forth was implemented in 1970 at the National Radio Astronomy Observatory (NRAO), where it was used to control an 11-meter radio telescope near Tucson, AZ, and to perform real-time data acquisition and analysis.

Because computers were extremely primitive in those days, Forth was designed with efficiency in both size and performance as an important objective. However, because NRAO was a research establishment with rapidly changing requirements, Forth was also designed to be inherently interactive and easy to program.

Many astronomers who visited the NRAO facility requested copies of Forth to use at their own research facilities. Impressed by its popularity, Moore and his colleagues Elizabeth Rather and Ned Conklin formed FORTH, Inc. in 1973. Since then, FORTH, Inc. has developed and sold software products based on Forth, and has provided custom programming services in Forth to a wide range of clients and in many application areas.

By the late 1970s, Forth had become sufficiently popular that a Forth Interest Group was formed. Standards were passed in 1979 and 1983, and an ANSI standard was adopted in 1994 followed shortly thereafter by an equivalent ISO standard.

The current standard is Forth-2012 and is available at forth-standard.org.

Today, Forth is available from numerous sources for virtually all popular operating systems and processors, from 8-bit microcontrollers to 64-bit workstations. Although Forth is not as ubiquitous as C, there are thousands of Forth programmers all over the world who value the language for its efficiency and its contribution to their productivity.

Forth is being used in a wide variety of application areas by government agencies such as NASA; by major corporations such as General Electric, General Dynamics, Lockheed-Martin, and Federal Express; and by countless small- and medium-sized businesses for whom it represents their competitive edge.

Reference The paper "The Evolution of Forth" gives in-depth details of Forth's history: www.forth.com/resources/evolution

1.2 The Philosophy of Forth

Forth expert Wil Baden[1] supplied the following definition of Forth to the committee

---

1. Wil Baden's home page (along with his alter ago "Neil Bawd") is at: http://home.earthlink.net/~neilbawd/

working on an ANSI standard for the language:

"Forth is a language for direct communication between human beings and machines. Using natural language diction and machine-oriented syntax, Forth provides an economical, productive environment for interactive compilation and interpretation of programs, low-level access to computer-controlled hardware, and the ability to extend the language itself."

Wil's discussion of this paragraph was interesting, and we include it here:

The first sentence tries to capture the general spirit of Forth. The second sentence gives the six most important features of Forth:

Using natural language diction and machine-oriented syntax...

All computer languages claim to use natural language diction. (Diction is what you find in dictionaries.) Forth encourages you to choose real and complete words — not words with scattered parts of their insides removed. Forth does this better than COBOL; the prolixity of COBOL syntax makes programmers economize in their choice of identifiers. In other languages, restrictions on the length of identifiers force the prgmr to mmbl. This is the basis for the power of Forth — making it easy for the computer to understand what you say saves precious resources for more profitable activity.

Forth provides an economical and productive...

The economy of Forth is its first, last, and greatest attraction. That's why Forth excels when resources are scarce, and is why programmers are attracted to it. Productivity keeps them there.

...environment...

Forth is not just a language, it's an environment. You and the language become one and invade the machine. Forth is the principal research, development, and production tool for Forth applications.

...for interactive compilation and interpretation of programs,

Forth is the most interactive of programming languages. Programming and checkout are not separate phases, but are intermingled in one interactive sharing.

low-level access to computer-controlled hardware,

Assemblers and other languages can get at the innards of machines, but not with the immediacy of Forth.

and the ability to extend the language itself.

Forth is a living language. You do not build or assemble applications. You grow them.

1.3 Course Hardware & Software

This course is based on SwiftForth, a product of FORTH, Inc., running under Windows, Linux, and macOS.

SwiftForth is a 32-bit Forth implementation, meaning the basic unit of data (single-precision numbers, addresses, etc.) is 32 bits wide. In Forth, this is called a *cell*.

However, we've attempted to identify all Forth issues that depend on features of FORTH, Inc. products, and write all student problems such that they can be worked on any Standard Forth system, as described in the next section.

1.4 Typographic Conventions

Certain typographic conventions are followed in this notebook. Executable Forth commands and source code are shown in a monospaced, bold typeface:

DECIMAL

If the input parameters to a command are described generally rather than given explicitly, they are shown in a monospaced typeface inside brackets:

`<number of milliseconds>` **CONSTANT MotorDelay**

Where we show data, such as strings being entered or examples with computer output, the data and/or output is shown in monospaced type. Commands you type are bold, but the computer responses are not:

1024 VALUE ROOMSIZE ok

A line of input you type at the Forth command line is always terminated by the Enter (or Return) key. In cases where there is some ambiguity, we may indicate the point at which you hit the Enter key with `<cr>`.

ROOMSIZE . `<cr>` 1024 ok

SwiftForth is by default not case-sensitive,[2] although some system-dependent things (such as Windows API calls and Linux file names) are case-sensitive. You may see some commands in upper or lower case in this and other books; except where noted, both upper and lower case forms are valid.

Throughout this text, we will note wherever possible when words and features are specific (though possibly not exclusive) to FORTH, Inc. products. Most words used here are either defined in Standard Forth or are in widespread use (e.g., **DEFER**, Section 7.1). However, the fact that a word is in the Forth standard doesn't necessarily mean all Standard Forth systems include it, because the Standard is structured with a required "Core" word set and a number of optional word sets. A compliant system may document which, if any, optional wordsets it includes. So, if a word you're looking for appears not to be in the system you're using, consult its documentation.

---

2. Case sensitivity is a user option in SwiftForth. Its default setting is case-insensitive.

1.5 Some Definitions of Terms

Forth allows any kind of character string to be a valid name, so certain ambiguities can arise. For instance, Forth subroutines are referred to as *words*, but *word* can mean an addressable unit of memory. To resolve this we will use certain conventions when speaking of common items:

- An 8-bit unit of data is called a *byte*. For purposes of this book, a byte is considered the same as a character, although we know in some circumstances characters are of other sizes.
- The word-length of the processor (e.g., 16 or 32 bits) is called a *cell*. This is also the size of an address and of a single item on a stack.
- On a 32-bit processor, a 16-bit item may be referred to as a *half-cell*.

Each type of value has its own operators, as you will find in the next section.

Section 2: Forth Fundamentals

2.1 Interaction with Forth

Forth is designed to promote intimate communication between you and the computer. The process of working with Forth is intended to be natural, unencumbered by complex syntax or by the necessity to change programs and environments during the programming process. This section describes basic elements of this process.

2.1.1 Communicating with Forth

The element of communication with Forth is the *word*, a string of non-blank characters. Words are separated from each other by one or more spaces (or "white space characters" in text files). You interact with Forth by typing a word or a group of words and then pressing the Enter or Return key (denoted in this text as <cr>).

For example, try saying[3] the following to Forth:

Try this
```
FORTH
123 .
.S
```

What you have done is to execute several words. The word is the basic executable unit in the Forth language. There are two general types of words:

- *Primitives*, characterized as machine dependent.
- *High-level words*, defined in terms of primitives and other high-level words.

When you use a word, it doesn't matter whether it is a primitive or high-level word, but internally they have very different characteristics.

Examples of primitives:

```
DUP    DROP    +    */
```

Examples of high-level words:

```
FORTH    QUIT    INTERPRET    .S    DUMP
```

Try typing DUP DROP <cr> and then FORTH <cr>. Is there any difference?

2.1.2 The Command Line

You can type multiple words and parameters on a single Forth command line. All

---

3. By "saying" we mean "typing at the Forth command line."

the keys you type are echoed on the command line and are saved for future interpretation, with a few exceptions:

- *Backspace* (or *Delete)* erases the character at the cursor position.
- *Enter* (or *Return)* terminates command line input, making the received text available for interpretation.

If you try to use a word Forth does not know — for example, **DIFFICULT** — Forth displays that word followed by an error message, such as a single question mark.

When you press the Enter key, Forth will process your command line in strict left-to-right order. Numbers will be placed on the stack, and words will be executed. If a word will expect one or more parameters, you must type them before the word so they'll be on the stack when the word executes.

Try this　　　**20 7 + . <cr>**

When processing this line, Forth will do the following:

1. Convert 20 to binary and push it onto the stack.
2. Convert 7 to binary and push it on the stack, above the 20.
3. Execute **+** which adds the two numbers together, removing both from the stack and leaving only the sum.
4. Execute **.** (pronounced "dot") which takes the top number off the stack, converts it to characters, and types it out.

Arithmetic operators such as **+** will be discussed more in Section 2.5.

SwiftForth includes some additional command-line features:

Table 1: Command-line features of SwiftForth:

Key	Action
PageUp PageDown	Scroll through the history of the current session.
Up and Down Arrows	Retrieve commands you have typed.
Left and Right Arrows	Move the cursor on the command line.
Insert	Toggle the insert/overwrite mode of typing.
Enter	Execute the command line the cursor is on.
Ctrl-C	Copy selected text.
Ctrl-V	Paste text at the insertion point.
Double-click	Selects the word under the cursor, making it available for the right-click and copy functions.
Right-click	Displays a pop-up menu of options to perform on the selected word or at the cursor position.

2.2 Data Stack Operations

Consider the concept of stacks for a moment.

- Of what use is a structure in which only one item at a time is available?
- What would happen if you had a large number of these items and needed one that was in the middle somewhere?
- If you needed the second item would you have to throw away the first item?
- What about double-precision numbers or boundary markers?

Although C and other languages frequently use stacks, they are usually treated as an internal resource and are not available to the programmer.

Most of us need practice working with stacks in order to appreciate them. We need to learn methods for manipulating items on the stack prior to examining the stack's role in handling formulas and argument lists. Many of the problems in the first few chapters of this book help you practice using Forth's stacks.

2.2.1 Stack Architecture

Push-down stacks provide a common means of passing parameters to subroutines ("words" in Forth). There are two push-down stacks in a Forth implementation.

1. The *data stack* holds numbers and the addresses of words and data. This is the most visible and directly accessible stack, and the one we mean when we refer simply to "the stack."
2. The *return stack* is normally used for nesting in Forth procedures, but may also be used for convenient temporary storage of numbers or addresses. Return stack use is discussed in Section 2.6 and Section 3.6.6.

These stacks are LIFO (Last In, First Out) lists, and are best visualized as items listed from left to right, where the right-most item is the top of the stack. For example, if we describe the stack as containing *n1 n2 n3,* we mean there are three numbers on the stack, with *n3* being on top (most accessible).

To remove and display the top cell of the data stack, use the Forth word **.** ("dot"). This will remove the top stack item and print its value. To see what is on the data stack without removing any items, use the Forth word **.s**.

Try this   Try entering this series of numbers: **1 2 3 4 5**

Which is the top item? Which is the bottom?

SwiftForth displays the current stack in a status line at the bottom of the command window.

Sometimes a word you're testing may leave several numbers on the data stack. It would be convenient to remove these numbers without having to type **.** over and over. To do this, type **xxx**, or any other undefined word. Now what's on your stack?[4] This happened because, when Forth couldn't find that word, it executed the standard **ABORT** routine described in Section 8.5.1.

Rule   The general rule for stack usage in Forth words is that a word removes its arguments from the stack and leaves only explicit results.

2.2.2 Stack Notation

The descriptions of Forth commands presented in this book include a comment to show what stack items are expected as input arguments and what results will be returned on the stack. An in-line comment such as this starts with a (followed by a space, and ends with a). For more information on comments, see Section 2.3.4.

The notation in these stack comments places input items to the left of a dash, and output items to the right. The rightmost item on either side of the dash is the top-most item on the stack, reflecting the fact that when we typed a list of numbers the last one we typed was on top. Some examples are:

(_n1 — n2_)   When this command executes, it will take the number _n1_ off the stack and leave a number _n2_ on the stack.

(_— n1 n2_)   This command takes nothing off the stack, but leaves the two new numbers _n1_ and _n2_.

(_n —_)   This command takes a number _n_ off the stack, but doesn't return anything.

(_—_)   This command has no effect on the contents of the stack.

The stack notation shown in Table 2 is often used to indicate the nature of items on the stack.

Table 2: Notation to indicate the kind of stack elements

Item	Meaning
addr	address
char	character (or byte)
d	signed double number
ud	unsigned double number
len	length (usually of a string)
n	signed number
u	unsigned number
flag	Boolean flag (-1 = true, 0=false)
x	single cell of unspecified type
xt	execution token

---

4. Some systems require a special word to clear the data stack. Consult your system documentation.

Where there are multiple items of a particular type on the stack, they are distinguished by indexes (e.g., *x1 x2*). In some special circumstances, additional notation may be used for clarity.

A stack comment describes only the use of the data stack by the word being documented. It doesn't imply anything about the absolute state of the stack. For example, the stack comment (–) means this word expects nothing and leaves nothing; it won't change the stack's state. This does not imply that the stack is empty. It is generally inappropriate to expect any absolute state of the stack, beyond the items a word expects or leaves. If words worry only about their own arguments and results, they have the useful property of being "context independent"; that is, they work the same, regardless of the absolute state of the stack, as long as their explicit parameters are provided. Always make sure the words you write follow this basic rule of stack usage. This will help you write more error-free code.

Now that you understand stack notation, we can describe a few of the words we've used in examples so far, in a glossary. You'll see more glossaries as we go along.

Glossary

FORTH $(-)$

Selects the "vocabulary" (list of available words) containing basic Forth commands.

.S $(-)$

Displays whatever numbers are on the stack without changing the stack (also called a non-destructive stack display).

DUP $(x - x\,x)$

Duplicates the top stack item.

DROP $(x-)$

Discards the top stack item.

+ $(n1\ n2 - n3)$

Adds the top two numbers on the stack, leaving the sum.

. $(n-)$

Converts the top number from binary to a string of numeric digits and displays it. ("dot")

2.2.3 Single-Cell Stack Manipulation Operators

The diagrams in this section illustrate the behavior of some common Forth words used to manage data items on the stack. The glossary that follows lists common stack operators with their definitions.

Figure 1. Stack operator DUP

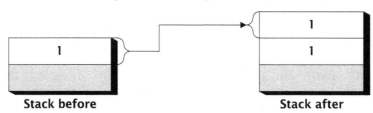

Figure 2. Stack operator DROP

Figure 3. Stack operator SWAP

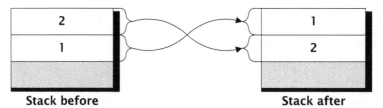

Figure 4. Stack operator OVER

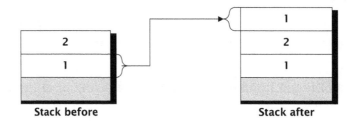

Figure 5. Stack operator ROT

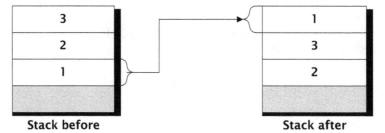

DUP $(x - x x)$

Duplicates the top stack item

DROP $(x -)$

Discards the top stack item.

SWAP $(x1 \ x2 - x2 \ x1)$

Swaps the order of the top two items.

OVER $(x1 \ x2 - x1 \ x2 \ x1)$

Copies the second stack item to the top.

ROT $(x1 \ x2 \ x3 - x2 \ x3 \ x1)$

Rotates the top three stack items to bring the third one to the top. (Pronounced "rote" — think of "rotate".)

−ROT $(x1 \ x2 \ x3 - x3 \ x1 \ x2)$

Rotates the top three stack items to send the top one to third place. ("minus-rote")

Note   **ROT** and **−ROT** work specifically on the top three stack items. They do not rotate the entire stack, nor will they work on other than three stack items.

The best way to understand the stack operator words is to put a few numbers on the stack and try them. Use **.S** to display the stack, if your Forth system doesn't automatically show it for you.

2.2.4 Double-Cell Stack Manipulation Operators

Similar operations work on pairs of stack items. A stack pair might be a double-precision number, XY coordinates, a string (address and count) or even two unrelated items.

You'll note that these words all begin with a "2". This is part of each word's name, a reminder that it deals with pairs of items. The "2" isn't a parameter, and you cannot invent **5DUP** just by typing its name!

In all cases, these operators will preserve the order of items within the pair, manipulating the pair as though it were one double-sized item. These operators are, of course, used with double-precision numbers, but they are equally useful with other number pairs such as the address and length of a string, and on any occasion when it's more convenient to manage stack items two at a time.

The diagrams in this section illustrate the behavior of some common words used to manipulate double-cell items on the stack. The glossary that follows lists common double-cell stack operators with their definitions.

Figure 6. Stack operator 2DUP

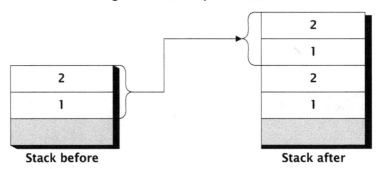

Stack before   Stack after

Figure 7. Stack operator 2DROP

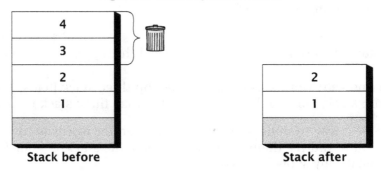

Stack before   Stack after

Figure 8. Stack operator 2SWAP

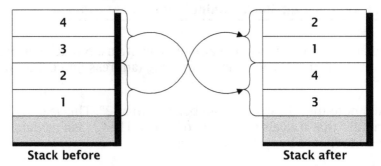

Stack before   Stack after

Figure 9. Stack operator 2OVER

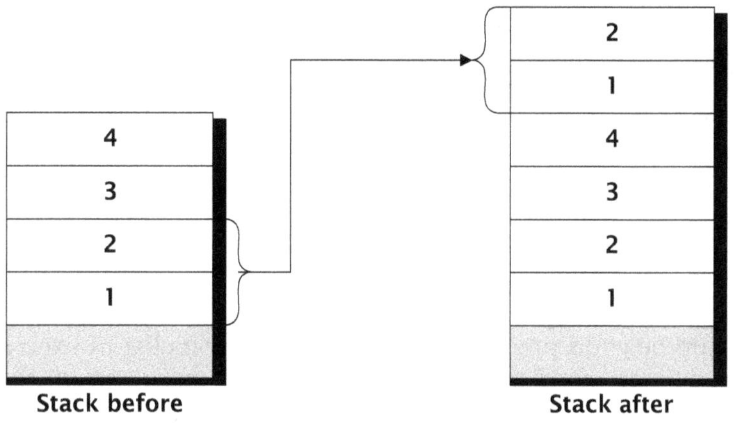

Stack before	Stack after

Glossary

2DUP
$$(x1 \ x2 - x1 \ x2 \ x1 \ x2)$$
Duplicates the top pair of stack items.

2DROP
$$(x1 \ x2 -)$$
Discards the top pair of stack items.

2SWAP
$$(x1 \ x2 \ x3 \ x4 - x3 \ x4 \ x1 \ x2)$$
Swaps the top two pairs of stack items.

2OVER
$$(x1 \ x2 \ x3 \ x4 - x1 \ x2 \ x3 \ x4 \ x1 \ x2)$$
Copies the second pair of stack items to the top.

2.2.5 Problems

In the problems below, show the operations needed to make the stack picture on the left (*input*) look like the one on the right (*output*). Some problems have more than one solution.

Table 3: Stack-operation exercises

Input	Output	Operations (answers here)
1 2 3	3 2 1	
1 2 3	1 2 3 2	
1 2 3	1 2 3 3	
1 2 3	1 3 3	
1 2 3	2 1 3	
1 2 3 4	4 3 2 1	
1 2 3	1 2 3 1 2 3	

Input	Output	Operations (answers here)
1 2 3 4	1 2 3 4 1 2	
1 2 3	(stack empty)	
1 2 3	1 2 3 4	
1 2 3	1 3	

2.2.6 Some Reflections

It would be good practice to review the previous list of exercises and see if you can think up a set of circumstances that would require each of the possible transformations.

For example: **1 2 3** to **1 2 3 1 2 3**
This could be required if the three top items were a boundary set and a constant.

Perhaps items 3 and 2 are the XY coordinates of a point in a graph and item 1 is its intensity, or maybe it's a three-dimensional graph.

Certainly, in a language where almost all the operations you can perform on numbers happen on a stack and leave something other than you started with, being able to duplicate the top several items is essential. What do you think is the likelihood of having to deal with more than three items? Can you think of any more stack operators that would be useful?

Forth is one of very few high-level languages to make a stack directly available to the programmer, and for this reason, many people who are new to Forth find it alien. However, it has some advantages:

- It saves having to define a lot of variables that are used only for temporary storage.
- It saves the cycles required to fetch and store values, as in many Forth implementations the top stack items are in a register or otherwise are readily available.
- It gives Forth the characteristic of being concatenative, a fancy word that means you can add an operation to a prior sequence of operations that left a value on the stack simply by doing it; you don't have to fetch the value again, or re-arrange parentheses, or re-order an "equation."

People who have learned Forth report that learning to use the stack comfortably was a lot like learning to ride a bicycle: it feels wobbly and awkward at first, but at some point it's like a switch being thrown in your brain. Suddenly it becomes intuitive and natural. Once that happens, you'll wonder why it ever felt so hard!

A primary objective of the first several chapters in this book is to help you get to that point. In a five-day course, most people find it happens sometime Wednesday!

2.3 Forth Definitions

2.3.1 Our First Forth Word

Before we proceed, let's make a Forth word that extends the system and acts in a user-friendly manner.

The syntax for this is very simple:

```
: <name>    <some other Forth words> ;
```

Let's make a word that says "HELLO." To do this, type the following sequence on the Forth command line exactly as it appears here:

Try this

```
: GREET   CR ." HELLO" SPACE ;
```

Now type **GREET** and watch what happens.

Relating this to other programming languages, the word **:** ("colon") is a subroutine-defining term similar to the procedure or function declarations used in other languages. The argument to the **:** is the name **GREET**, and the sequence of operation is to first send a **CR** (carriage return) to the terminal, then to output the string **HELLO.**

Please notice the space after **."** ("dot-quote") but not before the delimiting **"**. The reason is that **."** is a word, and words are separated from each other by spaces, whereas the final **"** simply marks the end of the string.

Finally, **GREET** prints a **SPACE** and then returns to the calling program.

What happened to the word **GREET** after we defined it? Forth translated the definition into an executable form and put it into a place called the *dictionary* (the details of this important data structure are discussed in Section 8.1). This process is called *compiling*. This happens every time you use **:** (or other *defining words* discussed later) to make a new word. Whenever you use a word, Forth will look at the end of the dictionary (the most recent word defined) and search backwards trying to find the word. If the word is found, it will be executed; if it can't be found, Forth stops and gives an error message.

When Forth is compiling a definition (i.e., everything following a **:** and name until the concluding **;**), it compiles references to words instead of executing them. The form of the reference depends on the Forth implementation. When the compiler encounters a number, it compiles it as a literal. A definition may only reference previously defined words; "forward references" are not allowed (although in certain limited circumstances you can achieve that effect using techniques discussed in Section 7.2.

Note that every word defined with a **:** must also have a name (**GREET** in this case) and an ending **;**. Even though a word consisting of only these three things wouldn't actually do anything, it does have uses, as we shall see later.

2.3.2 Rules for Word Naming

Unlike other programming languages, Forth supports names that consist of almost any combination of characters you wish to use.

This provides extremely flexible naming conventions. For example, in a financial package one might have words called **+DEBITS** to add a column of numbers and **%RATE** to calculate interest on a loan.

These names may be as long as 255 characters. They may contain upper- and lower-case letters, numbers, control codes or special characters (for example, ***(?!@** is a valid name). Although control codes may be used to name a word, we don't recommend using them, as some of these characters do strange things to terminals and printers, and they can make text difficult to view and edit. Also, be careful of names that look like valid numeric input!

Forth words can't contain spaces (which act as delimiters between Forth words), or any control characters that directly control the command-line input process (e.g. *backspace, delete, return/enter*).

Question   Are the following hypothetical words valid or invalid names?

```
12.45
SNEED
FLOW-RATE
TELESCOPE
PI+34+46/16
A2+2AB+B2
!!!!!!!
```

2.3.3 Compiling Forth Source

Every Forth implementation has some way of managing definitions in source form on disk that can be compiled. Early Forths used the concept of 1024-byte "blocks" of source, displayed as 16 lines of 64 characters each, with an internal mechanism mapping blocks to disk sectors or OS files. Most modern Forths, including Swift-Forth, use text source files. Here we will briefly describe SwiftForth's approach; if you are using a different implementation, consult its documentation. As you write more complex definitions to solve problems in this book, we recommend that you edit your work in files.

SwiftForth lets you use any text editor (e.g., Notepad or a programmer's editor) to prepare your source. You can also type definitions directly into SwiftForth's command window. If you wish, you can copy the text of a definition from the command window to a file or vice versa. If you have source in a file, you may direct Forth's text interpreter to it with the **INCLUDE** command.

```
INCLUDE <filename>
```

...causes Forth to interpret the text in that file as if it were being typed in the command window. The only difference is that, when interpreting from a file, SwiftForth will ignore whitespace characters such as *Tab*.

For more information on using SwiftForth with source files, see the *SwiftForth Reference Manual* supplied in PDF format with the SwiftForth system.

2.3.4 Programming Tools

Before we go much further, let's look briefly at some words found in all FORTH, Inc. products (as well as in many other Forths) that help you examine the system you're running on as well as your own code and data structures.

Glossary

DUMP   (*addr u* —)
> Display *u* bytes of memory, starting at address *addr* (generally formatted for output as hex digits, but may vary by system).

LOCATE <name>   (—)
> Display the source (if available) for word *name*.

SEE <name>   (—)
> Display the actual compiled code for word *name*.

Other programming aids are available on most systems; consult your product documentation for details.

Always remember, though, that the best debugging aid in Forth is Forth's own interactivity. You don't need test harnesses, single steppers, or debuggers to test your words. All you have to do is supply stack arguments and type a word's name to execute it. If you keep your definitions short, you will find it incredibly easy to test your code thoroughly.

Your definitions should all have stack comments, plus other comments to indicate usage and other information. The following commands support comments in Forth. Each of these is a Forth word, and must be followed by a space.

Glossary

((—)
> Begin a comment terminated by a **)**. It can span multiple lines, and can appear inside or outside a definition. Text within the comment will be ignored.

.((—)
> Like **(**, but the text will be displayed when the file is interpreted.

{   (—)
> Like **(**, but terminated by **}**. This allows parentheses to appear within the comment.

****   (—)
> Begin a comment terminated by the end of the line on which it appears.

\\   (—)

Ignore all following text until the end of the file.

2.4 Single and Double-Precision Numbers

The size of a single-precision number, a single stack item, and an address are always the same in Standard Forth. This size is called the *cell size* (in Forth we use the term "cell" to avoid confusion with "word," as the latter has other special meanings in Forth). Forth is available in 16-bit, 32-bit, and 64-bit cell versions. The 16-bit cell size is typically used with microprocessors and microcontrollers whose native cell size is 8 or 16 bits, and is used in FORTH, Inc.'s SwiftX cross-development systems for 8-bit and 16-bit targets.

On 32-bit systems (such as PCs and many embedded microcontrollers and microprocessors), single-precision numbers are 32-bits wide and there is less need for double-precision math. Similarly, a 64-bit implementation would have 64-bit single-precision numbers. For maximum portability across all implementations, however, Forth provides the same set of single, double, and mixed-precision operations on all systems regardless of cell size, and number conversion follows the same rules.

Because our classroom computers are typically 32-bit systems, we will throughout this book describe numbers assuming a 32-bit architecture.

2.4.1 Range of 16- and 32-bit Numbers

Unless floating-point hardware exists or special requirements arise, all math in Forth uses integer arithmetic operators. This means whole numbers only. On one hand, the loss of floating decimal and engineering notation may be an inconvenience; on the other hand, it's not a terrible loss because the trade-off in speed and simplicity is enormous when no hardware floating point is available. Forth is widely used in embedded applications on small microcontrollers, which rarely have hardware floating point. The performance advantage provided by integer arithmetic over software floating point is especially important in real-time applications.

In fact, many of the numbers we're accustomed to thinking of as fractions can be thought of as integers with different units. For example, we may consider a millivolt as a unit itself, rather than a thousandth of a volt. Similarly, we may consider money in cents rather than dollars and hundredths of dollars.

With this in mind, we need to consider the sizes of:

* Signed 16-bit integers: -32768 to 32767
* Unsigned 16-bit integers: 0 to 65535
* Signed 32-bit integers: -2,147,483,648 to 2,147,483,647
* Unsigned 32-bit integers: 0 to 4,294,967,295
* Unsigned 64-bit integers: 0 to 18,446,744,073,709,551,615

To act on these numbers, Forth has special math operators for each kind. These specific operators ensure speed and non-ambiguity.

2.4.2 Valid Single- and Double-Precision Numbers

Single-precision numbers are represented by strings of digits that represent numbers in the current number radix (typically found in the variable **BASE**). A leading minus sign is the only "punctuation" allowed.

This means that -12345 is valid on a 16-bit system; 123456 is valid on a 32-bit system, but not on a 16-bit system. ABCD is invalid in decimal, but is valid in hex.

Question   Are these valid or invalid numbers on the system you're using?

1234   3.1415   345678   1,234   1982   AD   DOG   YES 76999

Double-precision numbers may have a preceding minus sign but are distinguished from single-precision numbers because they have other punctuation.

Standard Forth specifies that a number with a decimal point to the right of the rightmost digit will be converted as a double-precision integer. FORTH, Inc. products also allow other punctuation for readability and convenience; any of the characters { + . , / : } and – (anywhere but the leading position) cause the number to be interpreted as double-precision. These are valid double-precision numbers:

```
111-22-3333
1,234,610
1.00,234
555-1212
12:27:32
7/23/48
```

Double-precision numbers take up two stack cells, where single-precision numbers only use one. The high-order cell is on top of the stack.

In the last section, we said that a word in Forth can contain, among other things, any combination of numbers. You might be wondering how Forth can differentiate between the two. For now, we will just tell you that if a word isn't recognized, it will be treated as a number; if that doesn't work, an error message is given. This is discussed in more detail in Section 6.1 and Section 8.3.

2.5 Arithmetic Operations

Arithmetic in Forth is done using *postfix notation*, which means that operands (e.g. numbers) precede operators (such as **+**). This is the most convenient method to use when working with stacks. Complex functions can be written and solved without the use of parentheses and, due to the nature of integer math, calculations are very fast. A large set of math operators is provided, some of which are listed below.

2.5.1 Simple Math Operations

Common standard single-, double-, and mixed-precision operations are shown in the following glossary.

Note that although Forth has distinct data types (e.g., single- and double-precision numbers), along with operators appropriate for each, it doesn't automatically select operators, enforce your selection, or otherwise interfere with the programming choices you make. You may have a valid reason for wanting to add a single to a double, or a number to a character's value. But you are responsible for keeping track of the types of data on your stack and for using operators that will do what you want.

Glossary

+	$(\ n1\ n2 - n3\ )$
D+	$(\ d1\ d2 - d3\ )$
M+	$(\ d1\ n - d2\ )$

Add the top two numbers, returning the sum.

-	$(\ n1\ n2 - n3\ )$
D-	$(\ d1\ d2 - d3\ )$

Subtract the top number from the second, returning the difference.

NEGATE	$(\ n1 - n2\ )$
DNEGATE	$(\ d1 - d2\ )$

Returns the two's complement (negative) of the number on the stack.

ABS	$(\ n1 - n2\ )$
DABS	$(\ d1 - d2\ )$

Returns the absolute value of the number on the stack.

MAX	$(\ n1\ n2 - n3\ )$
DMAX	$(\ d1\ d2 - d3\ )$

Returns the greater of two signed numbers.

MIN	$(\ n1\ n2 - n3\ )$
DMIN	$(\ d1\ d2 - d3\ )$

Returns the smaller of two signed numbers.

*	$(\ n1\ n2 - n3\ )$
M*	$(\ n1\ n2 - d\ )$
UM*	$(\ u1\ u2 - ud\ )$

Multiply two numbers, returning the product.

/	$(\ n1\ n2 - n3\ )$
M/	$(\ d\ n1 - n2\ )$

Divide the first number by the second (i.e., top stack item), returning the quotient.

/MOD	$(\ n1\ n2 - n3\ n4\ )$
UM/MOD	$(\ ud\ u1 - u2\ u3\ )$

Divide the first number by the second, returning the remainder and quotient (top stack item).

MOD   (*n1 n2 — n3*)

Divide the first number by the second, returning only the remainder. There is no mixed-precision version of this operator.

*/   (*n1 n2 n3 — n4*)
M*/   (*d1 n1 n2 — d2*)

Multiply the first two numbers together, divide by the third, returning the result.

The following glossary lists some simple operators implemented to act upon single-precision numbers in the most machine-efficient manner.

Glossary

1+	(*x1 — x2*)
2+	(*x1 — x2*)
CELL+	(*x1 — x2*)

Add one, two, or the number of bytes in one cell (depends on the target CPU's cell size) to the top stack item.

1-	(*x1 — x2*)
2-	(*x1 — x2*)
CELL-	(*x1 — x2*)

Subtract one, two, or the number of bytes in one cell from the top stack item.

2*	(*n1 — n2*)
2/	(*n1 — n2*)

Multiply or divide the top stack item by two.

CELLS	(*n1 — n2*)

Multiply the top stack item by the number of bytes in one cell.

Most of the unusual operators in Forth are designed to take advantage of computer architecture. For example, most machine multiplication operators leave a double-length product, and most division operators divide a double by a single. By combining them, ***/** gives you extra precision at very low cost. Similarly, most division leaves both a quotient and remainder; **/MOD** makes both available to you from a single division operation. Simple operators like **1+** and **1-** take advantage of increment and decrement instructions, while **2*** and **2/** are usually implemented as left and right arithmetic shifts, respectively.

Try this   **SEE 2***

...to disassemble the code for **2*** so you can see how it is implemented. Try this with some of the other operators listed above, too!

2.5.2 Scaling

Sometimes you may be asked to multiply two values, say A and B, and divide by another, C.

One could try A B ***** C **/**, but that might give a wrong answer in some cases. Why?

Scaling operators like ***/** are used to conserve precision. Given A B C on the stack, ***/** performs the following steps:

1. First multiply A by B, yielding a double-precision intermediate result,
2. then divide the result by C, yielding a single-precision once again.

This operator is used any time a number must be multiplied by a fraction or ratio.

2.5.3 More About */

Among the most obvious of all applications for scaling is the calculation of percentages. Given that a percentage can be defined as a fraction, one can define a **%** operator that would return the integer percentage required.

Try this   First try to define a word called **%** with the following stack picture:
(*n1 n% — n2*)

Pretty easy! After all, one only has to perform the following sequence to obtain 10% of 12300:

    12300 10 100 */

How would you calculate 105% of 12300?

2.5.4 Rational Approximation

The concept behind this useful technique is that any irrational constant (that is, numbers like π that cannot be exactly represented but potentially have an infinite number of decimal places) can be represented by a rational approximation with an error of less than 10E -8. As a convenience, a table of rational approximations is reprinted below.

As an example, calculate the circumference of a circle. The formula is two times the radius times π. Looking in the table below, we find that the value of π can be approximated by 355/113. The formula can now be stated as:

    r 2* 355 113 */ .

Try this   **5000 2* 355 113 */ .**

Table 4 shows a handy table of rational approximations[5] for various constants.

Table 4: Rational approximations of irrational numbers

Constant	Number	Approximation	Error
π	3.141 …	355/113	8.5 x 10-8
$\sqrt{2}$	1.414 …	19601/13860	1.3 x 10-9
$\sqrt{3}$	1.732 …	18817/10864	1.4 x 10-9
e	2.718 …	25946/9545	2.0 x 10-9
$\sqrt{10}$	3.162 …	27379/8658	6.7 x 10-10
$^{12}\sqrt{2}$	1.059 …	18904/17843	3.9 x 10-10
$\log_{10}2/1.6384$	0.183 …	2040/11103	1.3 x 10-8
ln2/16.384	0.042 …	846/19997	1.2 x 10-8
.0001°/22-bit rev	0.858 …	18118/21109	1.7 x 10-9

5. Hart, John F., *et al.*, *Computer Approximations*, Krieger Publishing Co., Inc.

Table 4: Rational approximations of irrational numbers

Constant	Number	Approximation	Error
arc-sec/22-bit rev	0.309 ...	9118/29509	3.3 x 10-9
c	2.9979248	24559/8192	1.6 x 10-9

2.5.5 Division

By now you may have noticed there are no multiply or divide operators for double-precision numbers. Rather than creating a D/ or D*, we use the mixed-mode scaling operation M*/. It works like this:

Given da b c on the stack, first multiply da by b, yielding a triple-precision intermediate product. Then divide the result by c, yielding double precision once again.

2.5.6 Example: Horner's Method of Polynomial Evaluation

Given any arbitrary polynomial, it may be factored for easier solution. After the factoring, integer math will be sufficient for calculation. For example:

$x^5 + 4x^4 + 8x^3 - 12x^2 - 6x + 17$

...may be factored as follows:

$x(x^4 + 4x^3 + 8x^2 - 12x - 6) + 17$

$x(x(x^3 + 4x^2 + 8x - 12) - 6) + 17$

$x(x(x(x^2 + 4x + 8) - 12) - 6) + 17$

$x(x(x(x(x + 4) + 8) - 12) - 6) + 17$

To calculate this answer using Forth, define a word like this:

```
: POLY ( n1 -- n2 )   DUP 4 +   OVER * 8 +
   OVER * 12 -   OVER * 6 - *   17 + ;
```

2.6 Return Stack Operations

We now know something about mixed-mode operators, so let us go back and examine how the operator */ might be implemented. Remember, */ generates a double-precision intermediate product, then uses a single-precision divide to produce a single-precision result. This could be accomplished by using M* and M/.

Try this Try defining */ in terms of those operations and notice what the stack problems are. The problem is clearly what to do with the denominator.

This is not an unusual occurrence. Forth is equipped to handle situations where getting a stack item out of the way for a moment would be perfect, by letting you use its *return stack*.

The return stack is not just used for temporary storage. Its principal use is for nesting return addresses for definitions made by the word **:** ("colon"), hence its name.

For purposes of saving and restoring parameters, the following operators support limited use of the return stack:

Glossary   Note the use of "R:" to denote the return stack picture.

>R
$$(x -) (R: - x)$$
Takes the top item off the data stack and pushes it onto the return stack.

R>
$$(- x) (R: x -)$$
Pops the top item off the return stack and pushes it onto the data stack.

R@
$$(- x) (R: x - x)$$
Pushes a *copy* of the top return stack item onto the data stack.

2>R
$$(x1 \ x2 -) (R: - x1 \ x2)$$
Takes the top item off the data stack and pushes it onto the return stack.

2R>
$$(- x1 \ x2) (R: x1 \ x2 -)$$
Pops the top item off the return stack and pushes it onto the data stack.

In the example a * (b+c), where the stack picture is (*b c a*), the return stack could be used this way:

```
>R + R> *
```

Warning!   What goes on the return stack in a definition must come off the return stack before the **;** at the end of the definition[6] is reached. Also, these operators are only legal inside colon definitions.

Try this   Now define ***/** using the return stack.

2.7 Problems

1. What is the average of the following six numbers?

```
123.
400
1,000,998
3
65534
1
```

2. In the problems below, rewrite the equations using postfix notation and the proper

---

6. Or before an early EXIT is reached. We'll learn more about EXIT later.

arithmetic operators.

Table 5: Exercise — math equations in Forth

Equation	Forth Code
12 + 12	
123 * 15	
1.234 + 3.14	
123 + 1.00000	
123 * (16 / 4)	
10000. * 15 / 36	
((15 * 123) - 64 + 32) / 6	

3. What is 2 to the 6th power?
4. Round a number with one decimal place (e.g., 21.3) to the nearest integer.
5. Round a number with one decimal place to the nearest integer that is evenly divisible by two.
6. Make the single-precision item on the stack into a double-precision item.
7. How would you do the following operations if you had the unknowns on the stack?

Table 6: Exercise — algebra

Input	Formula	Code
A	$3A^3 + 4A^2 - 5A + 10$	
A B	(A + B) + 1	
A B	3A - 2B + 2	
A B	A + B(A + B)/2	
A B	.5AB/100	
A B	(A+B) * (A-B)	
A B C	(A*(B+C)+A)	
A B C	$A^2 + 2AB + B^2 + C$	

Hint for the algebra-challenged: $(A+B)^2=A^2+2AB+B^2$

8. Define words to convert temperatures, using these formulas:

```
°C = °(F - 32) / 1.8
°F = (°C * 1.8) + 32
°K = °C + 273
```

Express all arguments and results in whole degrees, without rounding. Use these names:

```
F>C
F>K
C>F
C>K
K>F
K>C
```

Edit your definitions into a file. Each definition should have this stack picture:

(*n1 — n2*)

...where *n1* is the input in one set of units, and *n2* is the output in the converted units. Test your words with the following values:

- 0°F in Centigrade
- 212°F in Centigrade
- -32°F in Centigrade
- 16°C in Fahrenheit
- 233°K in Centigrade
- -40°C in Fahrenheit

Section 3: Structured Programming in Forth

3.1 Introduction

The concept of structured programming was introduced by Dutch computer scientist E.W. Dijkstra and his colleagues[7] in the early 1970s. Structured programming provides a uniform way to break a complicated structure into simple parts.

Seen from a high level, structured programming is often (but not always) associated with a "top-down" approach to design.

At a low level, structured programs are restricted to simple, hierarchical program-flow structures. These are *concatenation*, *selection*, and *repetition*:

- *Concatenation* refers to a sequence of statements executed in order.
- In *selection*, one of a number of statements is executed depending on the state of the program.
- In *repetition*, a statement is executed until the program reaches a certain state or operations are applied to every element of a collection.

Each program structure should have only one entry point and one exit point. The use of arbitrary branching (as with a GOTO statement) is not permitted.

Forth's architecture strongly encourages adherence to these principles, both in high-level and assembler. This chapter focuses on the flow-of-control issue.

3.2 Conditionals

IF is the selection or conditional word in Forth. It is rather different in operation from other languages' conditional structures, which are characterized by something like the following syntax:

```
IF A = B THEN ... ELSE ... CONTINUE
```

In the above example, statements following THEN will be executed if A and B are equal, or the statements following ELSE will be executed if A and B are not equal. The traditional syntax may be read like this:

"*IF* A and B are equal *THEN* do this stuff, *ELSE* do this other thing and then *CONTINUE*."

Most programming languages have some form of this statement though the actual syntax differs among them.

In Forth, an equivalent statement would be as follows:

7. O.J. Dahl, E.W. Dijkstra, C.A.R. Hoare. *Structured Programming*, Academic Press, London, 1972 ISBN 0-12-200550-3

```
A B = IF ... ELSE ... THEN
```

Scripting this line in Forth would go something like this:

"Are A and B equal? *IF* they are, do this; *ELSE* do that; *THEN* go on with what you need to do next."

3.2.1 Using Conditional Structures

The basic form of a conditional structure in Forth is:

```
<flag> IF  <words for true case>
    optional:  ELSE <words for false case>
    THEN <program continues>
```

IF is a destructive word: it removes the top stack item and uses it as a flag. If it is *any* non-zero value, the words immediately following **IF** are executed. If it is zero, words following an optional **ELSE** are executed, and **THEN** is the point at which unconditional execution continues.

Glossary

IF   (*flag* —)
If *flag* is true (non-zero), execute the words that follow; otherwise branch to the words following **ELSE** (or following **THEN** if there's no **ELSE**).

ELSE   (—)
Begin an optional false clause in an **IF** ... **THEN** structure. Words following **ELSE** will be executed if the value passed to **IF** is zero.

THEN   (—)
Terminates a conditional structure that begins with **IF**. Note: every **IF** must have exactly one **THEN** in the same definition.

Try this   Type this definition:

```
: TRY ( x - )  DUP IF  ." True value "
    ELSE ." False value " THEN . ;
```

Use the word by typing:

```
<n> TRY
```

...where *n* is any number. What happens?

Remember that your value must be on the stack before you execute **TRY**.

Now use your new word to test the following operations:

```
-1 TRY
0 TRY
1 TRY
```

What happens?

Try these examples:

```
12 12 - TRY
123 0 MAX TRY
-123 123 MIN TRY
123 0= TRY
0 INVERT TRY
```

How does the - get used as an operator for comparison? What logical operation is performed? What did **INVERT** do?

It is not necessary to have both a true clause and a false clause; the false clause (beginning with **ELSE**) is optional. However, every **IF** must have a **THEN** to terminate the structure. It's "bad form" (inefficient and less readable) to have only a false clause; if you're tempted to do that, invert the condition before **IF** using **0=** or **NOT** (described in the next section) so that you have only a true clause.

Important | **IF**, **ELSE**, and **THEN** (as well as all other "structure" words in Forth) should only be used *inside* colon definitions. This is because these words are active during the process of compilation and they direct the formation of the compiled statement.

The comparison operators (which we'll get to shortly) and all Forth stack and math operators — in fact, any words that leave a number on the data stack — are good input to **IF**.

3.2.2 Nesting IF Structures

IF structures may be nested arbitrarily deeply, providing you nest an entire structure within the next outer structure. You may not use an **IF** to branch out of or into another structure. We strongly recommend that you avoid nesting too deeply, as this can lead to unreadable, unmaintainable code.

If you are testing for a list of conditions, consider using a **CASE** statement (discussed in Section 3.3).

3.2.3 Comparison and Logical Operators

The Forth comparison operators are easy to use and are also postfix, just like the math words. They remove items from the stack and return a flag that **IF** (or any other word) can use. Here is a list of them (plus some other useful words) and their behaviors:

Glossary | **Single-operand operators**

0<   ($n - flag$)

Returns true if n is less than zero.

0> $(n — flag)$

Returns true if *n* is greater than zero.

0= $(n — flag)$

Returns true if *n* is zero, false for non-zero.

D0= $(d — flag)$

Returns true for double-precision zero.

NOT $(flag1 — flag2)$

Returns true for zero, false for non-zero.

INVERT $(x1 — x2)$

Inverts all the bits in *x1* to give *x2* (its one's complement).

Note the difference between **NOT** and **INVERT**: **NOT** is a *logical* (Boolean) operator that treats the entire flag as true/false. **INVERT** performs a *bitwise* operation.

Glossary   **Double-operand operators**

= $(x1\ x2 — flag)$

Returns true if *x1* and *x2* are equal.

<> $(x1\ x2 — flag)$

Returns true if *x1* and *x2* are not equal.

> $(n1\ n2 — flag)$

Returns true if *n1>n2*.

< $(n1\ n2 — flag)$

Returns true if *n1<n2*.

D< $(d1\ d2 — flag)$

Returns true if *d1<d2*. Note double-number comparison.

U< $(u1\ u2 — flag)$

Returns true if *u1<u2*. Note unsigned comparison.

AND $(x1\ x2 — x3)$

Bitwise AND operator.

OR $(x1\ x2 — x3)$

Bitwise OR operator.

XOR $(x1\ x2 — x3)$

Bitwise exclusive-OR.

Glossary   **Miscellaneous useful operators**

?DUP $(x — x\ |\ x\ x)$

Duplicate top stack item only if it is non-zero. This is useful preceding **IF** when you need a copy of the value in the true part but not the false part (it saves an **ELSE DROP**). Note that the stack comment uses a vertical bar on the right side to indicate alternative results.

WITHIN (*n1 n2 n3 — flag*)

Returns true if n1 ≥ n2 and *n1* < *n3*. Note that the range is inclusive on the low end and exclusive on the high end.

TRUE (*— flag*)

Returns a true flag (-1).

FALSE (*— flag*)

Returns a false flag (0).

Try this   Write words to do the following:

TEST *n* greater than 0 and less than 32767.

TEST *n1* and *n2* equal to zero.

How would one simplify these expressions?

Try doing a more complicated problem:

Is *n1* greater than 32 or less than 127?

How does this work out? There is help for us in a single word that tests for a number within a range. It is appropriately called **WITHIN** and is described in the glossary entry above.

Try this
```
50 32 127 WITHIN
0 32 127 WITHIN
127 32 127 WITHIN

: RANGE ( n -- )   500 1000 WITHIN  IF ." In range"
    ELSE ." Out of range" THEN ;
```

Tip   When you're first learning to use the stack, you may find it helpful to format your definitions vertically, showing stack effects on each line. For example:

```
: RANGE ( n -- )\ n
    500 1000 \ n 500 1000
    WITHIN\ t
    IF \ [stack empty]
    ." In range" \ Print if t TRUE
    ELSE
    ." Out of range"\ Print if t FALSE
    THEN ;
```

As you get more accustomed to using the stack, you may find a less vertical style easier to read, and priority in your comments should be directed at explaining the logic of your code.

3.3 Case Statements

A high-level case statement is available for situations in which an input condition needs to be checked against more than one or two possible values. The syntax is shown in Figure 10.

Figure 10. CASE statement syntax

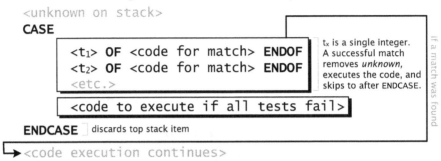

The structure begins with **CASE**, which requires a case selector *x* on the stack. A series of **OF** ... **ENDOF** clauses follows, each **OF** preceded by a comparison value on the stack. The case selector is compared against the test values, in order. If a match is found, the case selector is dropped from the stack and the code following the successful **OF** is executed, up to its terminating **ENDOF**. Execution then continues after the **ENDCASE**. If the case selector does not match any of the test values, it remains on the stack after the last **ENDOF**, and some default action may be taken. *Any default action should preserve the stack depth* (use **DUP** if necessary), because **ENDCASE** performs a **DROP** (presumably on the case selector) before continuing execution.

The **CASE** structure is flexible, and is more readable than nested **IF** statements if there are more than two or so comparisons. As with all Forth control structures, **CASE** statements may be nested; there may be any number of **OF** ... **ENDOF** pairs; and there may be any amount of logic inside an **OF** ... **ENDOF** clause. However, if the logic in an **OF** ... **ENDOF** clause is complex, we recommend factoring it into a separate definition to facilitate testing.

Glossary

CASE   (—)
Begins a structure that is terminated by **ENDCASE**, which may have any number of **OF** ... **ENDOF** clauses between **CASE** and **ENDCASE**.

OF   (*x1 x2 — x1* |)
Begins a conditional clause in a **CASE** ... **ENDCASE** structure. If *x1* = *x2*, removes both values from the stack and executes the words between **OF** and **ENDOF**. Otherwise, retains *x1* on the stack and continues after the **ENDOF**.

ENDOF   (—)
Terminates a conditional clause begun by **OF** and transfers to the location following **ENDCASE**.

ENDCASE   (*x —*)
Terminates a structure that is begun with **CASE**, discarding a value (presumably an "unknown" not consumed by a successful **OF**).

Try this   Here's an example:

```
: TEST ( n - )
   CASE  ." Value is "
      1 OF ." One" ENDOF
      2 OF ." Two" ENDOF
      3 OF ." Three" ENDOF
      DUP .
   ENDCASE ;
```

Try it with various values of *n*. Why is the **DUP** necessary in the next-to-last line?

3.4 Problems

1. Define a word that will return true if the top two stack items are both zero.
2. Define a word that will display the phrase "VALID CHARACTER" if *n* is a printable character. You can use 32 to 127 as the range of printable characters.
3. Define a word that will leave the value *n* on the stack if *n* is not equal to zero. You could show the stack effect as (*n* — *n* |), where the vertical bar character | separates the stack effect in the true case from the false case.
4. Define a word that will return false if any of the following values equals *n*, otherwise returns true:

   15, 10, 5, 0

5. Define a word named **MAXIMUM** (without using the standard word **MAX**) that accepts two parameters from the stack, compares them, retains the larger, and discards the smaller.

   MAXIMUM is used in the following way:

   ```
   1 2 MAXIMUM
   2 1 MAXIMUM
   ```

   After **MAXIMUM** is executed, the larger of the two numbers is on the stack.

3.5 Indefinite Loops

Indefinite loops are a natural extension of conditionals. In the following, it is important to remember that selection of the most appropriate structure will simplify your code.

Forth has two indefinite looping structures:

> **BEGIN** ... <flag> **UNTIL**

...and...

> **BEGIN** ... <flag> **WHILE** ... **REPEAT**

Like the **IF ELSE THEN** structure, these must be used inside colon definitions. Like **IF**, **UNTIL** and **WHILE** consider any non-zero value of *flag* to be true.

Simply stated, these loops work until some condition is met. They are considered useful for applications where an indefinite number of iterations must be performed before being terminated by some event. This could be a key being struck, or a timer going off, or perhaps a boundary being approached.

These two loops fall under the classical definitions of *pre-test* and *post-test* loops.

3.5.1 Post-testing Loops

The Forth post-testing loop structure is:

```
BEGIN  <words to be repeated>  <flag> UNTIL
```

For example:

```
: DOWN ( n -- )  BEGIN  ." VALUE IS"  DUP  . CR
  1- ?DUP 0= UNTIL ;
```

This structure performs its test at the end of the loop: "do it until this happens." It executes all the statements between the BEGIN and the UNTIL at least once. When UNTIL sees a true *flag* on the stack, it will exit the loop and continue to the next statement.

Here's a similar example that counts up:

```
: UP ( n -- )  BEGIN  ." VALUE IS"  DUP  . CR
  1+ DUP 10 = UNTIL DROP ;
```

Note that DOWN is able to use ?DUP (which only duplicates non-zero values) because it's waiting for a zero, but UP has to do a DROP after the loop exits.

Question Consider this definition:

```
: FOREVER ( - )  BEGIN 0 UNTIL ;
```

If you execute this word, will the loop ever terminate? If no, why not? If yes, under what circumstances?

3.5.2 Pre-testing Loops

The form of an indefinite loop that performs its test before performing the repeatable operation is:

```
BEGIN  <words executed at least once>  <flag> WHILE
    <words executed while flag is true>  REPEAT
```

This structure provides a loop that can execute "zero" times, by putting the test between BEGIN and WHILE and executing the words between WHILE and REPEAT only if the argument to WHILE is true: "Do it while this condition is true."

Here are examples similar to the ones in the previous section, but using a pre-testing loop. Note that if your argument to these is the same as the value you're testing for (0 and 10, respectively), you will get no output:

```
: DOWN ( n -- )   BEGIN  ?DUP WHILE
   ." VALUE IS " DUP . CR  1- REPEAT ;
```

...and:

```
: UP ( n -- )   BEGIN  DUP 10 < WHILE
   ." VALUE IS " DUP . CR  1+ REPEAT DROP ;
```

3.5.3 Infinite Loops

A closely related type of loop, the **BEGIN ... AGAIN** loop, provides an infinite loop — one for which there is no exit condition.

```
BEGIN   <words to be repeated indefinitely>  AGAIN
```

An infinite loop is useful for specifying the natural behavior of a system, that is, the highest-level definition in an application. The behavior of a background (or "control") task is usually defined this way. A typical task assignment might look like:

```
: RUN ( -- )   SAMPLER ACTIVATE  INITIALIZE
   BEGIN  SAMPLE  RECORD  1 #SAMPLES +!  AGAIN ;
```

...where **SAMPLER** is the name of a task, and the rest is part of the application.

Question   How is **BEGIN ... AGAIN** different from **BEGIN ... 0 UNTIL**?

3.5.4 Indefinite Loop Words

Glossary

BEGIN   (—)
Begins a structure that is terminated by **REPEAT, UNTIL,** or **AGAIN.**

WHILE   (*flag* —)
Begins the conditional part of a **BEGIN ... WHILE ... REPEAT** structure. Executes the words between **WHILE** and **REPEAT** so long as *flag* is true (non-zero). Exits the structure by branching to the point following **REPEAT** when *flag* is false.

REPEAT   (—)
Terminates a **BEGIN ... WHILE ... REPEAT** structure with an unconditional branch to the word immediately following **BEGIN.**

UNTIL   (*flag* —)
Terminates a **BEGIN ... UNTIL** structure. If *flag* is false (zero), repeats the loop from the word immediately following **BEGIN.** When *flag* becomes true (non-zero), it exits the loop.

AGAIN $(-)$

Terminates a **BEGIN** ... **AGAIN** structure with an unconditional branch to the word immediately following **BEGIN**.

3.5.5 Problem: ?WAY

Define a simple application to operate in the following manner:

- Set up an indefinite loop.
- On each pass through the loop, get the character value of a keystroke from the terminal.
- If it was the Esc key, leave the loop; otherwise, given the key value, perform the following conditional procedure.
- Process the key, generating output as shown for the key codes given in this table:

Key	Output
I	UP
J	LEFT
K	HOME
L	RIGHT
M	DOWN

- If the key was anything else, display the character.

Take care to factor this definition into clearly separate functions; the key to this is simplicity.

A good name for this is **?WAY** (pronounced "which way?").

In this problem, you'll need to use the following words (discussed in Section 5):

KEY $(-char)$

Awaits a character from the keyboard and returns its code.

EMIT $(char-)$

Displays the character whose code is *char*.

CHAR $(-char)$

Returns the code for the character that follows in the input stream. Generally used on the command line (or while interpreting a file), not inside colon definitions.

[CHAR] $(-char)$

Compiles a literal value of the code for the character that follows. Used only inside colon definitions. The character code is returned at run time.

<u>*Example*</u>   `: LETTER-A ( -- c ) [CHAR] A ;`

Note that you can use **KEY** interactively to find out what the character code for any letter is. For example, if you type:

```
KEY . <cr> I
```

You need to press <cr> to start executing **KEY**, which will wait for you to type the letter and then execute . to type out the value of the character code.

Alternatively, use **CHAR** to get a character code:

```
CHAR I . <cr>
```

In this case, **CHAR** parses the next token in the input stream and returns its character code, unlike **KEY**, which awaits its own input.

Optional Make **?WAY** handle both upper- and lower-case characters. This problem will expand later on, so do a good job!

3.6 Finite Loops

The next kind of control structure is the definite, or finite, loop. We use this kind of iteration technique when we know (or can calculate) how many times the loop must be performed, or at least the maximum number of times it must be performed.

The basic form of a finite loop in Forth is:

```
<limit> <index> DO <repeated words> LOOP
```

DO expects two items on the stack, the starting value of the *index* and a *limit*. These items are removed from the stack and are maintained internally (usually on the return stack). On each iteration, **LOOP** increments the index by 1 and compares it to *limit*; it exits the loop when *index* becomes equal to *limit*. If you need a copy of the current value of the loop index, you can get it by using the word **I**. Note that **I** is only available inside the loop, inside this definition.

There are good examples of this type of structure in Fortran and BASIC, and in most all other high-level languages. For example, to display the numbers between 0 and 10 in BASIC, one would use the following sequence of statements:

```
10 FOR I=0 to 10
20 PRINT I;
30 NEXT I
```

In Forth, the same effect (0 through 10, inclusive) would be accomplished by the following word:

```
: COUNT-UP ( -- )   11 0 DO  I . LOOP ;
```

Question What is the difference between these two structures? How many times is the iteration performed in each case?

Loop parameters are checked *at the end of the loop*, so any loop will always execute at least once, regardless of the initial values of its parameters. Because the parameters are checked at the end, and if the end condition is met the loop terminates immediately, it is necessary to use 11 in **COUNT-UP** to get the number 10 to display.

Because a **DO** loop with equal input parameters will execute not once but a very large number of times (equal to the largest possible single-cell unsigned number), the word **?DO** should be used in preference to **DO** if the loop parameters are being calculated and might be equal to each other. **?DO** will skip immediately to the end of the loop if the parameters are equal.

Following is a summary of the important words used in finite loop structures. Some of these are discussed in more detail in the following sections.

Glossary

DO
$(\ n1\ n2\ -\ )$
Begins a structure that is terminated by **LOOP**, using $n2$ as the starting value of the loop index and $n1$ as the limit.

LOOP
$(-)$
Compares the current value of the loop index with the limit, and exits the loop when they are equal. The index and limit are kept in an internal location, often the return stack.

?DO
$(\ n1\ n2\ -\ )$
The same as **DO**, but skips the loop entirely if $n1=n2$. This extra comparison and conditional transfer impose some extra overhead, so don't use them if you know $n1$ and $n2$ can't be equal.

+LOOP
$(\ n\ -\ )$
Increments the current value of the loop index by the signed value n. Exits the loop when the index passes the limit (they don't have to become exactly equal).

I
$(-\ n)$
Returns a copy of the current value of the loop index for the innermost **DO LOOP**[8] structure. May only be used inside a **DO LOOP** and within the same colon definition.

I'
$(-\ n)$
Like **I**, but returns the current loop limit. **I'** is a non-standard word that is in fairly common use. As such, it may not be available in all Forth implementations.

J
$(-\ n)$
Like **I**, but returns the current loop index for the next-outer **DO LOOP** structure.

LEAVE
$(-)$
Exits a **DO** ... **LOOP** immediately, to the point following the next **LOOP** or **+LOOP**. Usually used inside an **IF** ... **THEN** structure for an early exit when some exception condition has become true.

UNLOOP
$(-)$
Discards the current loop index and limit. Must be used if you leave the loop using **EXIT** rather than **LEAVE**.

---

8. For the purposes of this entire section, a **DO LOOP** refers to any structure that begins with either **DO** or **?DO** and ends with either **LOOP** or **+LOOP**.

It is important to remember that the finite loop words cannot be arbitrarily mingled with indefinite loop words. The important distinction is that a finite loop is maintaining a loop index and limit, whereas the indefinite loops have no such concept. For this reason, **I** inside a **BEGIN** ... **UNTIL** structure, for example, is meaningless, and you cannot use **LEAVE** to exit from an *indefinite* loop.

3.6.1 Index Access

The significant aspect of the **DO LOOP** in Forth is that the iteration control values are on the stack prior to the execution of the loop and are removed by the **DO** word.

Like the **IF ELSE THEN** and indefinite looping structures, the words **DO** and **LOOP** must be used within a colon definition because they direct the compiler. The parameters of the iteration do not have to come from within the same definition as the loop. You may pass the values to **DO** from the stack.

In the word **COUNT-UP** above, the execution would proceed as follows:

```
: COUNT-UP   11 0 DO  I . LOOP ;
```

1. The values 11 and 0 are removed from the stack by the **DO** and are established as the loop parameters, with 0 as the initial index and 11 the limit.
2. The commands between **DO** and **LOOP** are executed in order:
   I copies the current value of the loop index to the data stack.
   . ("dot") prints the value from the stack and removes it.
3. **LOOP** increments the current loop index by one. If the new index is less than the limit, it will begin again at the word following the **DO**. Otherwise it will exit.

How many times was the structure executed?

Question What is the smallest number of times you can make **DO LOOP** execute?

The reason for the order of the loop parameters — with the starting value on top of the stack and the limit beneath it — is because this makes it easy to structure a definition that will do something a number of times specified by a value that is on top of the stack. For example:

```
: TRYS ( n -- )   0 DO CR ." TRY " I . LOOP ;
```

The parameters to the word **DO** can be any pair of single-cell numbers.

Try this Here is an interesting experiment:

Define a word **COUNTS** that accepts its limit and index parameters from the stack and types out the current value of the loop counter on every iteration of the loop.

Now try giving it the following ranges:

- 100 90
- -50 -60
- -10 -20

- 0 -20
- 9 -20

What is the behavior of the **LOOP** test?

3.6.2 Counting by 2 or Other Values

There are times when one would like to count by a number other than +1. Can you think of a few examples?

To do this, Forth provides another kind of looping structure that uses the same **DO** word, but whose looping word takes a *signed increment* from the data stack.

That word is **+LOOP** and it is used in the form:

```
<n> +LOOP
```

...where *n* is the increment added to the loop counter, each time the loop executes, prior to the test for **+LOOP** termination. Note that *n* can be negative, so it is easy to construct a loop that counts down instead of up.

Try this   Define this word and execute it:

```
: +COUNT ( n -- )  0  DO I . 2 +LOOP ;
```

What is the behavior of this word?

Now here's a version that counts down:

```
: -COUNT ( n1 n2 -- )   DO I . -2 +LOOP ;
```

Here are some ranges you might try with **-COUNT**:

```
100  0
50  100
-50  25
0  100
```

Question   How is this **+LOOP** different from **LOOP**?

3.6.3 Premature LOOP Termination

There are times when it would be nice to stop a loop before the limit has been reached. This type of condition arises in process control when testing for a limit switch, or during pattern recognition problems when testing for matches or for convergence of a matrix operation. This is facilitated in Forth by the word **LEAVE**. When **LEAVE** is executed, the loop terminates immediately.

Question   How does **LEAVE** appear to operate? How would you construct such a word?

Sometimes you need not only to exit the loop, but to also exit the word in which the loop appears. This strategy should be used infrequently, because it violates one of the basic principles of structured programming — each routine should have only one entry and one exit. Multiple exits from a word should be avoided, in general, because they make the program flow harder to follow and your code more difficult to understand, debug, and maintain. But in situations when it would take a lot more code and complexity to avoid such an exit, the words **UNLOOP** and **EXIT** are useful.

The word **EXIT** causes Forth to leave a definition immediately, and to resume execution of the next word in the definition that called the word containing **EXIT**.

A trivial example of **EXIT** is:

```
: TEST ( n -- )  1 . IF EXIT THEN  2 . ;
0 TEST 1 2
1 TEST 1
```

However, if you use **EXIT** inside a **DO LOOP** structure, you can create a problem, because you would be leaving the loop parameters on the return stack. The word **UNLOOP** discards the loop parameters for the current nesting level of a **DO LOOP** structure. This word is not needed when **LOOP** completes normally (or via **LEAVE**), but it *is* required before leaving a definition by calling **EXIT**. One **UNLOOP** call for each level of loop nesting is required before leaving a definition.

Warning   If you find yourself using **EXIT** more than once in a word, you should consider refactoring it into two or more simpler definitions.

3.6.4 Problems

1. Define a word called **AVALANCHE** that accepts as input an unsigned single-precision number and computes "avalanche" numbers. The rules for avalanche numbers are:
 • If the number on the stack is odd, multiply it by 3 and add 1.
 • If the number on the stack is even, divide it by two.
 • If the number on the stack is one, stop.

 For example:

    17 AVALANCHE 52 26 13 40 20 10 5 16 8 4 2 1

2. Define a word called **RANGE** that takes a range of numbers and loops between those numbers until termination or until the iteration counter equals 50. Within the loop, just type out the current value of the loop index.

 For example:

 0 40 RANGE displays 0 1 2 … 39, and
 30 60 RANGE displays 30 31 32 … 50 (then stops).

3. Define a word called **STAR** that displays an asterisk character (*) on the terminal. (Hint: This might be implemented using either **EMIT** or ." which were introduced earlier.)

4. Define a word called **STARS** that displays <n> **STARS** upon request.

5. Define a word called **BOX** that displays a figure in the following manner.

   For example, **3 5 BOX** would display a box like this:

   ```
   *****
   *****
   *****
   ```

6. Define a word called **/BOX**, which produces a "slanted" box (Hint: **SPACE** outputs a single space and <n> **SPACES** outputs the given number of spaces.)

   For example, **5 4 /BOX** would display a slanted box like this:

   ```
       ****
      ****
     ****
    ****
   ****
   ```

7. Define **DIAMOND** so that it produces a diamond shape.

   For example, **5 DIAMOND** displays this:

   Warning: This is not easy!

3.6.5 Nested LOOP Structures

The following rules must be observed whenever you are using finite loops:

1. **DO** range values come from the stack. After **DO** gets them, they are removed and placed elsewhere (typically on the return stack), and when the loop terminates they are discarded completely.
2. **DO** always needs two parameters, although it does not care how they get there. Frequently the limit is supplied as a parameter to the word containing a loop.
3. **+LOOP** also requires a parameter every time it is executed.
4. If you **DUP** something inside a **LOOP** (to keep a copy because it would otherwise be consumed), it will be on the stack when the **LOOP** terminates. If you don't want it, **DROP** it before ending the definition.
5. The stack effect of the phrase inside the loop must be no net change. Otherwise, there is risk of stack overflow or underflow.

Assuming these rules are followed, you may nest loops arbitrarily deeply, and may use loops within other structures, or may include other structures inside loops. When nesting structures, *take care to nest entire structures*: you may not have structures that "straddle" other structures. For example, the sequence ... DO ... IF ... LOOP ... THEN is illegal and will not work.

In a nested DO LOOP, I always returns the current index for the innermost loop at the time I is executed.

Try this To test this, try the following:

```
: TRY ( -- )   10 0 DO  CR I . 2 SPACES
   20 0 DO  I . LOOP  LOOP ;
```

To get a copy of the next outer loop from within an inner loop, use the word J. If you need to nest deeper than that, you should factor your inner or outer loop into separate definitions to facilitate testing and maintainability.

3.6.6 Use of the Return Stack by DO and LOOP

We have noted previously that in most Forth implementations, DO removes its arguments from the data stack and pushes them onto the return stack. This is where LOOP or +LOOP will manipulate and test them. When the loop terminates, LOOP or +LOOP removes those arguments from the return stack.

Question Knowing this, can you understand why it's imperative that you not try to "jump out" of a loop?

Because of this behavior, you must obey some other rules when working with loops:

1. Both the beginning and ending of a DO LOOP structure must be inside the same definition.
2. LOOP or +LOOP are the only valid terminators for a structure beginning with DO or ?DO.
3. If you use >R or R> in the same definition as a DO LOOP, they must be either both outside or both inside the loop (and at the same level, if there are nested loops).

3.6.7 Picking the Best Loop Structure

Common guidelines advise you to use a *finite loop* if:

• You know (or can calculate) how many times you want to do it
• You know the maximum number of times you want to do it
• You need access to the loop index

...or use an *indefinite loop* if:

• You want to do it until some event occurs
• You want to do it while a condition exists
• You have no idea how long either of these intervals may persist

- You don't need a loop counter (loop index)

Using the most appropriate loop can result in simpler code and better performance.

3.6.8 Problems

1. Define a word **SIGMA** that works like this:

   <n> **SIGMA** returns the sum of all integers from 0 to *n*.

2. Define a word called **FACTORIAL** that does this:

   <n> **FACTORIAL** returns *n* factorial on the stack. For those who are not familiar with the factorial function, the rules are:

   - *n* is a positive integer.
   - 0 **FACTORIAL** is 1.
   - 1 **FACTORIAL** is 1.
   - Factorial, for which the mathematical notation is n!, has the following definition:
     n! = 1 * 2 * 3 * .... * (n-2) * (n-1) * n

3. Define a word called **RAMP** that could be used, for example, to control a stepper motor or robot arm. This word takes a single number as input, representing distance; and it generates that many values, which rise to a maximum amplitude, level off, and then decrease. Use 7 as the maximum amplitude.

   For example, **15 RAMP** would give:
   1 2 3 4 5 6 7 7 7 6 5 4 3 2 1 ok

   4 RAMP will give:
   1 2 2 1

   A good solution to this problem uses only one **LOOP**.

3.7 A Summary of Control Structures

Selection:

```
<flag> IF ... THEN
<flag> IF ... ELSE ... THEN
```

Indefinite iteration:

```
BEGIN ... <flag> UNTIL
BEGIN ... <flag> WHILE ... REPEAT
BEGIN ... AGAIN
```

Indefinite iteration with two exits:

```
BEGIN .. <flag> WHILE .. <flag> UNTIL .. THEN
```

Definite iteration:

```
<n1><n2> DO  ... LOOP
<n1><n2> ?DO ... LOOP
<n1><n2> DO  ... <n3> +LOOP
<n1><n2> ?DO ... <n3> +LOOP
```

Early termination of, or exit from, definite loops:

```
LEAVE
UNLOOP
```

Section 4: Data Storage

Up to this point, none of the exercises in this book have needed named data storage. We delayed introducing Forth constants and variables in order to ensure that you get plenty of practice designing routines *without* using named data items.

In other languages, you can't do much without naming data. In Forth, you can do quite a lot with just the stack. This is one of Forth's big sources of efficiency. But more complex applications usually require named data items and structures. Forth not only supports this, but offers a unique level of flexibility by allowing the programmer to define new *kinds* of data structures, which we'll get to in Section 8.6.

4.1 Single Data Objects

The two generic kinds of data objects are *variables* (named storage locations) and *constants* (named values). A third kind of data object has characteristics of both: it is a named *value* that can be changed, whereas constants cannot be changed.

4.1.1 Variables

The word **VARIABLE** defines a one-cell location in memory for data storage. **VARIABLE** is used in the following way:

    VARIABLE PLACE

...defines a variable named **PLACE**.

We may describe words like **VARIABLE** as having two *behaviors*: a *defining behavior* (which creates a member of this class of words), and an *instance behavior* that is shared by all words defined by **VARIABLE**.

These two behaviors of **VARIABLE** are as follows:

1. The defining behavior creates a dictionary header and allots one cell of data space.
2. When an instance (a word defined by **VARIABLE** such as **PLACE** in the example above) is executed, it pushes the address of its data space onto the stack.

Glossary   The following glossary lists defining words for different kinds of variables. Note the two different stack pictures: the first is for the *defining* behavior of the word itself and the second shows the stack effect for an *instance* of the defining word.

VARIABLE $(-)(-addr)$

Defines a word with one cell of data storage. When a word defined by **VARIABLE** is executed, it returns the address of its value.

2VARIABLE $(-)(-addr)$

Defines a word with two cells of data storage. When a word defined by **2VARIABLE** is executed, it returns the address of the first cell of its storage area.

CVARIABLE $(-)(-addr)$

Defines a word with one byte of data storage. When a word defined by **CVARIABLE** is executed, it returns the address of its storage area. **CVARIABLE** is typically available only on embedded systems, such as FORTH, Inc.'s SwiftX.

4.1.2 Access to Data Storage

The two things we must be able to do with data are fetch it from an address, and store it into an address. Each word in the **VARIABLE** class returns the address of its data storage.

Glossary Cell memory access operators:

@ $(addr - x)$

Fetch the one-cell value *x* from memory at address *addr*. Pronounced "fetch."

! $(x\ addr -)$

Store the one-cell value *x* to memory at address *addr*. Pronounced "store."

+! $(x\ addr -)$

Add the value *x* to the cell in memory at address *addr*. Pronounced "plus-store."

Glossary Prefixing these operators with 'C' (for "character") gives us these byte operators:

C@ $(addr - char)$

Fetch the *char* from memory at address *addr*. Pronounced "C-fetch."

C! $(char\ addr -)$

Store the one-byte value *char* to memory at address *addr*. Pronounced "C-store."

C+! $(x\ addr -)$

Add *char* to the byte in memory at address *addr*. Pronounced "C-plus-store." **C+!** is not a standard word and may not be available in all implementations.

Glossary Prefixing the cell operator names with '2' (for double) gives us these double-cell operators:

2@ (*addr — d*)

Fetch the two cells from memory at address *addr*. Pronounced "2-fetch."

2! (*d addr —*)

Store a two-cell value to memory at address *addr*. Pronounced "2-store." The top cell on the stack is stored in the first cell in memory.

For all the "store" operators defined above, the address is *always* on top of the stack. Therefore, if you have derived data from a complex process, all you need to do is say, for example, **EVENT !** to store that data in a variable named **EVENT**. Failure to put these arguments in the right order can be a fatal error.

Continuing with our example above, you could type:

```
1024 PLACE !
PLACE @ . 1024
```

The order in which the cells are managed is preserved in **2@** and **2!**. The high-order (i.e., the most significant) part of a double-length number is always on top of the stack, and the top stack item will be stored in the cell with the lower address in memory (the first cell).

The prefix letters are especially important, because they help you match the correct operator to each data type. Forth has distinct data types (characters, single-cell items, double-length items, etc.), but makes no attempt to enforce the matching of the various operators to specific data types. You can, for example, fetch individual characters or bytes from a **VARIABLE** (one cell):

```
VARIABLE DATA
DATA C@
DATA 1+ C@
```

Warning Individual access to the bytes of a variable depends on the byte order of the CPU. For example, many processors are little-endian (the least significant byte of data is at the lower address in memory) whereas others are big-endian.

Similarly, you can access the individual cells of a **2VARIABLE**:

```
2VARIABLE MORE-DATA
MORE-DATA @
MORE-DATA CELL+ @
```

This example does not have the byte-order dependency noted above. Further, using **CELL+** to increment the address by one cell can ensure that this usage is portable across systems of differing cell sizes.

However, most of the time you'll want to use **2@** and **2!** with instances of **2VARIABLE**, **C@** and **C!** with words defined by **CVARIABLE**, and so on. It is almost always an error to use a larger fetch or store operator with a smaller data type. For example,

```
DATA 2@
```

...will certainly fetch two cells, but you have no way of knowing what's in the cell that isn't part of **DATA** (which was defined as a single-cell variable above).

Tip A word that is particularly convenient for debugging is **?**, which queries a variable. It is usually defined as:

```
: ? ( addr - ) @ . ;
```

4.1.3 Constants

The defining word **CONSTANT** defines a class of words whose behaviors are as follows:

1. The *defining* behavior of **CONSTANT** (used to define members of the class) creates a header in the dictionary and compiles the number that is on top of the stack into the dictionary.
2. The *instance* behavior of **CONSTANT** (executed by members of the class) pushes onto the stack the number compiled when the instance was defined.

CONSTANT is used in the following way.

Try this
```
1024 CONSTANT 1K
1K . <cr> 1024
```

Note that you don't need any words, other than the instance name, to retrieve the value of a **CONSTANT**.

The word **2CONSTANT** is available to define a constant whose value may be either a double-precision value or two single-precision values, depending on your usage.

VALUE lets you assign a name to a number, like **CONSTANT** does, and later execution of that name leaves the assigned value on the stack. But the value can be changed with the word **TO** (whereas the value of a **CONSTANT** cannot be changed).

VALUE is used in the following way:

Try this
```
1024 VALUE ROOMSIZE
ROOMSIZE . <cr> 1024
2000 TO ROOMSIZE
ROOMSIZE . <cr> 2000
```

The choice between **VALUE** and **VARIABLE** is one of optimization and personal style, but the choice between **VALUE** and **CONSTANT** is more technical: a **CONSTANT** cannot be changed at run-time on most systems whereas a **VALUE** can. This may also affect how the compiler allocates storage for the value, especially in an embedded application with a mix of read-only code space and writable data space.

Glossary

CONSTANT   (*x* —)
                                                                                          (— *x*)

Defines a constant whose value is *x*.

2CONSTANT   (*x1 x2* —)
                                                                                          (— *x1 x2*)

Defines a two-cell constant whose cells hold the values *x1* and *x2*. (In the stack notation, these separate values may be specified as one double-precision value *d*).

VALUE   (*x* —)
                                                                                          (— *x*)

Defines a changeable constant whose initial value is *x*.

TO   (*x* —)

Changes the value of the **VALUE** whose name follows **TO** to *x*.

4.1.4 Some Words About Defining Words

Prior to this chapter, we had only one kind of "defining word," : (colon). Now we've introduced several others, and there will be more before this book is done. So let's take a few minutes to explore the concept of a "defining word" in Forth.

Consider a colon definition. The colon itself is a defining word, and it is followed by the name of a new definition. The *defining behavior* of colon creates a header in the Forth dictionary for the name, and compiles references to all the words following that name, up to the semi-colon that terminates the definition. The *instance behavior* of the new word defined by : (colon) executes the words compiled in the definition.

So, we can generalize a few things about defining words:

- Each defining word makes an instance of a specific *class* of words, with a class-specific defining behavior and instance behavior.
- A defining word is always immediately followed by the name of the instance being defined.
- The defining behavior creates a dictionary entry for the instance; it may do other things as well, such as allocate data space or compile code.
- The defining behavior may have a stack effect (e.g., the value assigned to a constant is consumed when the constant is defined).

Forth makes no distinction between "nouns" and "verbs," between data objects and functions. For example, instances of **VARIABLE** are executable, just as colon definitions are; the action of an instance of **VARIABLE** is to push the address of its data space onto the stack.

In the absence of scoping mechanisms such as *word lists* (discussed in Section 8.2), all words — including those defined by **CONSTANT** and **VARIABLE** — are global, and any data space assigned at compile time is static. A common mistake made by programmers learning Forth is to attempt to use defining words such as **VARIABLE** inside a colon definition, hoping to make their instances local to that definition. But defining words used inside a colon definition are just like other words in that definition: they will only be executed when the definition is *executed*, not when it is compiled! So, appropriate usage would be something like this, with the constant (or variable, or value, etc.) defined outside the colon definition:

```
1000 CONSTANT SIZE
: SHOW ( - )   SIZE 0 DO ...
```

4.1.5 Problems

1. In 1626, Dutch traders bought Manhattan Island from Indians belonging to the Wappinger Confederacy for fishhooks and other goods worth 60 guilders ($24 according to the 1626 exchange rate[9]). Suppose those clever Wappingers had deposited their $24 in the Bank of New Amsterdam at 5.5%. What would their investment be worth in 1926?

   • First do this problem using simple interest:

   amount = principal * interest rate * time

   • Then do it using compound interest, compounding annually (compute the simple interest every year and add it to the principal).

   Hint: Your numbers are going to get very large.

2. Your application needs a set of parameters called **UPPER-LIMIT**, **LOWER-LIMIT**, **STARTING-VALUE**, **CURRENT-VALUE**, and **INCREMENT**. All of these have fixed default values, but their actual values may change in use.

   Define these data items, and a user word **LIMITS** to set upper and lower limits, and sets **STARTING-VALUE** and **CURRENT-VALUE** to **LOWER-LIMIT**. Write a word **STEP** that will add **INCREMENT** to **CURRENT-VALUE**, and then display **CURRENT-VALUE**. If **CURRENT-VALUE** reaches or passes **UPPER-LIMIT** or **LOWER-LIMIT**, it should be reset to **STARTING-VALUE**. Include a word called **DEFAULTS** that re-establishes all the default values.

   You may define these items using **VALUE**, **VARIABLE**, or a combination of the two. If you wish, write this problem twice, once using **VALUE** and then using **VARIABLE**. Compare the resulting code.

4.2 Simple Arrays

An array is a named entity referring to more than one item of data. Arrays are commonly used to hold groups of numerical data or strings of text.

---

9. This is about 0.2 cents per acre. Historians estimate that the purchasing power of 60 guilders was equivalent to several thousand dollars. This still looks like a good deal until you realize that the Wappingers didn't actually own the island. They nonetheless set an example of business dealing that has inspired residents of the area to this day.

Glossary These words are used to define and manage arrays.

BUFFER: (*u* —)
(— *addr*)

Create a named array of length *u* bytes. Its instance behavior is to return the starting address of the array.

CREATE (—)
(— *addr*)

Creates a named data object associated with the next location in data space. Its instance behavior is to return the address of this data space. However, **CREATE** doesn't allocate any data space; this must be done with **ALLOT** or one of the other memory management words described later.

HERE (— *addr*)

Returns the address of the next available location of data space.

ALLOT (*n* —)

Allots *n* bytes of data space, starting at **HERE**.

Simple arrays may be built using the word **BUFFER:** preceded by a size in bytes and followed by a name. When the name is invoked, it will return the address of the beginning of the buffer. Equivalent results may be obtained by **CREATE** and **ALLOT**.

The following lines construct two identical arrays, each 100 bytes long:

```
CREATE STUFF   100 ALLOT
100 BUFFER: STUFF
```

The **CREATE** ... **ALLOT** sequence is just slightly more "manual," and the individual words in it can be used to build other kinds of structures as well.

The address and length of a region of memory form the principle arguments for words used to manage arrays:

Glossary

ERASE (*addr u* —)

Erases a region of memory (clears it to all binary zeros), given its starting address and length.

BLANK (*addr u* —)

Sets the specified region of memory to blanks (20H).

FILL (*addr u char* —)

Fills the specified region of memory with the least significant byte of *char*.

DUMP (*addr u* —)

Displays a formatted dump of the *u* number of bytes starting at address *addr*.

Try this The following example defines a buffer named **STUFF** that is **SIZE** (50) bytes in length. We then fill the buffer with various values and dump its contents.

```
50 CONSTANT SIZE
SIZE BUFFER: STUFF

STUFF SIZE 255 FILL
STUFF SIZE DUMP

STUFF SIZE ERASE
STUFF SIZE DUMP

STUFF SIZE 2/ BLANK
STUFF SIZE DUMP
```

4.2.1 Address Arithmetic

When using an array, it is frequently necessary to increment an address by the size of one cell. In order to have code easily transportable between implementations with different cell sizes, these words are available:

Glossary

CELLS (*n1 — n2*)

Multiplies *n1* by the number of bytes in a cell, to return the number of bytes in *n1* cells.

CELL+ (*addr1 — addr2*)

Adds the number of bytes in one cell.

CHARS (*n1 — n2*)

Multiplies *n1* by the number of bytes in a character, to return the number of bytes in *n1* characters.

CHAR+ (*addr1 — addr2*)

Adds the number of bytes in one character.

On a 16-bit implementation, you would expect to find something like this:

```
: CELLS ( n1 -- n2 )   2* ;
: CELL+ ( addr1 -- addr2 )   2+ ;
```

On a 32-bit system, the corresponding definitions might be:

```
: CELLS ( n1 -- n2 )   2* 2* ;
: CELL+ ( addr1 -- addr2 )   4 + ;
```

Get in the habit of using **CELLS** and **CELL+** to enhance the portability and readability of your code.

Analogous words **CHARS** and **CHAR+** are in Standard Forth for incrementing addresses by characters. That is important if you're writing code that may run on processors for which a character, a byte, and an address unit are not always the same size. Such platforms are rare, however, and if you accept the *environmental dependency* that these are the same size, you probably won't limit the portability of your code significantly. For the purpose of this book, we assume they are the same size.

4.2.2 Example: Array Manipulation

Let's create an array named **CATALOG** with space for five cells (elements).

We'll define a word named **ELEMENT** that, given a parameter *n* on the stack, returns the address of the *n*th element of the array.

You can store and fetch data from **CATALOG** using the index (0-4) of each **ELEMENT** in the array.

Finally, we'll define a word named **SHOW** that prints the entire array.

ELEMENT is used in the following way:

<n> **ELEMENT** (The address of the *n*th element is now on the stack.)

Here's the code:

```
5 CELLS BUFFER: CATALOG

: ELEMENT ( n -- addr )          \ Return addr of the nth element
    0 MAX  4 MIN                 \ Clip n to legal value
    CELLS CATALOG + ;            \ Get addr of nth cell

: SHOW ( -- )                    \ Display all five elements
    5 0 DO  CR ." Element " I . ." contains "
       I ELEMENT @ . LOOP
    CR ;
```

And here's a simple test for it:

```
: TEST ( -- ) 5 0 DO  I 5 * I ELEMENT ! LOOP ;  ok
TEST  ok
SHOW
Element 0 contains 0
Element 1 contains 5
Element 2 contains 10
Element 3 contains 15
Element 4 contains 20
ok
```

4.2.3 Problems

1. Create a word named **ARRAY** that will be used to define a class of arrays in the following way:
   <n> **ARRAY** <name>

   ...where *n* is the number of one-cell elements in the array and *name* is the name of the array.

ARRAY should create a header in the dictionary and allot the specified number of cells. Now write a word INDEX that expects a parameter on the stack that is added to the address of the array instance as an index into the array.

ARRAY is used in the following way:

```
10 ARRAY STUFF
4 STUFF INDEX
1 STUFF INDEX
```

2. Use ARRAY to define an array four cells in size. Make words that name each of the four cells. For example:

```
4 ARRAY ITEMS
```

After your definitions, FIRST returns the address of the 0th cell, SECOND returns the address of the next, etc.

4.3 Tables

A table is an array whose initial content is specified at compile time. A table definition usually starts with CREATE followed by one or more uses of , (pronounced "comma") or c, ("C-comma") to compile specific values.

The word , allots one cell of data space in the next available dictionary location and stores the top stack item in it. The most common use of , is to compile values into a table whose name and starting address is defined by using CREATE. Consider this example:

```
CREATE TENS  1 , 10 , 100 , 1000 , 10000 ,
```

This establishes a table whose starting address is given by TENS. It contains powers of ten from zero through four. Indexing this table by a power of ten will give the appropriate value. A possible use might be:

```
: 10** ( n -- 10**n )   CELLS TENS + @ ;
```

Given a power of ten on the stack, 10** will return the appropriate power of ten.

When a single-character-size amount of data is sufficient, c, performs a function analogous to , but for characters instead of cells. Normally this means either character codes or integers that fit in a character-sized memory unit (which is normally, but not always, a byte).

Section 5: Characters and Strings

5.1 String and Character Management

Forth provides many words used to reference single characters or strings of characters. Characters may be grouped together and thought of as a string; this group can then be operated on as a single entity.

5.1.1 Single Characters

It is frequently desirable to refer to a character code, for example, to specify a delimiter for a parsing operation. Forth provides two words for this purpose; they differ in that one is used inside a definition while the other is used interpretively (i.e., from the command line or in a source file outside a definition).

CHAR (— *char*)

Parse the word following **CHAR** from the input stream. Put the character code of the first character of this word on the stack. **CHAR** is normally used interpretively.[10]

[CHAR] (—)
(— *char*)

At compile time, parse the word following **[CHAR]** in the input stream and compile the value for its character code as a literal. At run time, that literal is returned on the stack.

Try this   For example, if you type:

    CHAR A

...you'll get the character code for the letter "A" on the stack. However, inside a definition, you might write:

    : ?DIGIT (char -- flag)   [CHAR] 0 [CHAR] 9 1+ WITHIN ;

...which returns true if the character supplied on the stack is a decimal digit. Specifying a character this way makes your code much more readable than simply plugging in the numeric code as a literal, and because **[CHAR]** compiles the character code as a literal, there's no difference in program size or performance.

But this strategy is only practical with visible graphic characters. If you're working with control codes, we recommend defining them as constants, such as:

    27 CONSTANT ESC

Many Forth systems, including those from FORTH, Inc., define **BL** to return the code for the space character ("blank") because that character is so frequently used.

---

10. Or inside a colon definition that needs to parse a character code from the input stream and then do something with it.

5.1.2 Strings

Forth contains several words used to reference strings, compare them, and move them between different locations. In addition, other words are used for string input and output.

Most words that operate on exactly one string of characters expect the length of that string to be on top of the stack with its address beneath:

    (addr u -)

Words that operate on two strings expect three or four items on top of the stack:

    (addr1 addr2 u -)
    (addr1 u1 addr2 u2 -)

In the first stack picture above (three arguments), the single length u applies to both of the strings instead of using two separate character counts. In the second stack picture (four arguments), a length is given for each string.

Glossary   The primary string management words are shown in the following glossary:

MOVE   (*addr1 addr2 u —*)
Moves u bytes from source *addr1* to destination *addr2*. This move ensures that the destination always contains all the information originally at the source, even if the address ranges overlap.

CMOVE   (*addr1 addr2 u —*)
Moves u bytes from source *addr1* to destination *addr2*. Like **MOVE**, but the move proceeds from low to high addresses.

CMOVE>   (*addr1 addr2 u —*)
Like **CMOVE**, but starts transferring at high memory and works toward low memory. Pronounced "c-move back."

/STRING   (*addr1 u1 n — addr2 u2*)
Adjusts the string *addr1 u1* by n characters, giving $addr2 = addr1 + n$ and $u2 = u1 - n$.

-TRAILING   (*addr u1 — addr u2*)
Shortens the string *addr u1* by stripping any trailing blanks that may follow the last non-blank character.

Two examples of string move commands are diagrammed below. These figures show the difference in operation between **CMOVE** and **CMOVE>** and the effects of text movement. In both cases the strings overlap, as shown in the following figures.

Figure 11. Moving strings with CMOVE

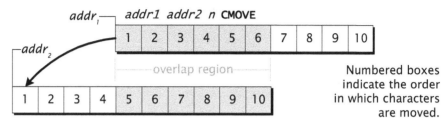

Figure 12. Moving strings with CMOVE>

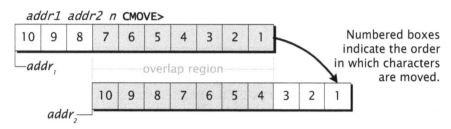

Question What would be the effect of using **CMOVE>** on the strings overlapped as in Figure 11 above? Or of using **CMOVE** on the second pair? Draw a picture.

The word **MOVE** tests for overlap, then uses either **CMOVE** or **CMOVE>** to do the string move. Most of the time you will use **MOVE**, unless you're interested in the following special behavior of the **CMOVE** words. (**PAD** is described in Section 5.1.3.)

Try this
```
PAD 80 ERASE
HEX
DEADBEEF PAD !
DECIMAL
PAD DUP 4 + 76 CMOVE
PAD 80 DUMP
```

Explain the result. When might this trick be useful?

5.1.3 String Scratchpad

A standard working area is used to hold most character strings for processing. This area is of indefinite size, and its location in memory usually is defined as an offset from the current top of the dictionary.

Executing the word **PAD** returns the address of this working area. Because **PAD** usually is located relative to the dictionary, any operation that reserves or releases dictionary space, such as **VARIABLE** or **ALLOT**, may change the location of **PAD**, rendering any data left there inaccessible; therefore, **PAD** is best used only for temporary operations, not for storing strings for later use. **PAD** provides a convenient way to supply an address for many of the string operators described in this section.

PAD (— *addr*)

Returns the address of a scratch pad that may be used for temporary storage of strings (or other data).

5.1.4 Counted Strings

Many Forth words that manage strings use an internal format called a *counted string*. This format stores the string's length (up to 255) in the first byte:

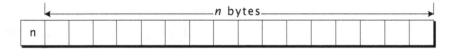

This format is more efficient than a "null-terminated string" (common in other languages) because the count is stored when the string is acquired, and doesn't impose a run-time penalty of re-counting the string every time it is used or of testing for the null terminator.

COUNT is frequently used with counted strings. **COUNT** takes as its parameter the address of a counted string. It returns the address of the string's first character and the length of the string:

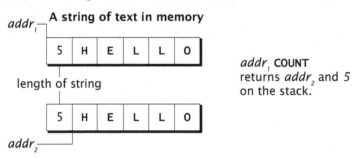

COUNT (*addr1 — addr2 u*)

Takes the address of a counted string and returns the address and length of the string itself (i.e., excluding the leading count).

The following is a simple definition that expresses the behavior of **COUNT**:[11]

```
: COUNT ( addr1 -- addr2 u )   DUP 1+ SWAP C@ ;
```

---

11. This is just an example. The actual implementation of **COUNT** is usually done in assembler to take advantage of the CPU's instruction set.

5.1.5 Character and String Input

Glossary   These words provide for string input from a user input device, such as a keyboard:

ACCEPT   (*addr u1 — u2*)
Awaits up to *u1* characters from the current user input device, placing them at *addr.* Input is terminated by a CR (e.g., the Enter or Return key). **ACCEPT** returns the actual count *u2* of characters received. If more than *u1* characters are sent, the excess characters are discarded.

KEY   (*— char*)
Waits for a single character from the input device and leaves its character code on the stack.

KEY?   (*— flag*)
Returns true if a character is available to be returned by **KEY**.

EKEY   (*— u*)
Waits for a single keyboard event on the input device and leaves its value on the stack. The encoding of keyboard events is implementation defined.

EKEY?   (*— flag*)
Returns true if a keyboard event is available to be returned by **EKEY**.

Note that **KEY** returns a character code in the implementation-defined character set. In the old days of serial terminals, that was usually just a 7-bit ASCII code. But more complex input terminals and PC environments have made that inadequate.

A more general word capable of returning *any* keyboard event (including control codes and function keys) is **EKEY**.

Both **KEY** and **EKEY** will wait until a key (or keyboard event) is available. If you want to ask whether a new **KEY** or **EKEY** is available, the words **KEY?** and **EKEY?** can be used; these tests are non-destructive. When either returns true, a subsequent use of **KEY** (after **KEY?**) or **EKEY** (after **EKEY?**) will retrieve the incoming character or keyboard event without waiting.

Try this
```
: TRY ( -- )  BEGIN  EKEY? IF
        EKEY DUP 27 = IF  DROP EXIT
      ELSE . CR THEN THEN AGAIN ;
```

Exercise this definition, typing a mix of letter keys and function keys. Now try the same definition using **KEY?** and **KEY** instead of **EKEY?** and **EKEY**. How does its behavior differ?

The word **ACCEPT** is the main word used by Forth to receive its input stream from the keyboard. Because **ACCEPT** will immediately respond to any "editing" characters such as **BS** and **DEL** it encounters (by backspacing in the string), and because **CR** (Enter or Return) will terminate input, this behavior makes **ACCEPT** unsuitable for communications or for receiving binary data across a serial line. For these purposes, we recommend **KEY** or **EKEY** in a loop.

5.1.6 Character and String Output

Just as Forth has both single-character and multi-character words for input, it also has two for output:

TYPE (*addr u —*)

Outputs *u* characters from *addr* to the output device.

EMIT (*char —*)

Takes one character from the top of the stack and sends it to the output device.

Try this Output a single character:

65 EMIT

Output a string of characters:

PAD 10 65 FILL
PAD 10 TYPE

5.1.7 String Problems

1. Define **INSERT** (*n char —*) so that the character on top of the stack is inserted into the counted string at **PAD** after character *n*.
2. Define **DELETE** (*n —*) so that the *n*th character is deleted from the counted string at **PAD** and the string at **PAD** is shortened accordingly.
3. Define **UPPER** (*char1 — char2*) to convert lower-case character codes to upper case, and define **LOWER** to do the opposite.

5.2 Scanning Characters to a Delimiter

Glossary These two words are available for parsing text:

WORD (*char — addr*)

Using *char* as a delimiter, skip leading delimiters and parse until the trailing delimiter is found or until the input stream is exhausted. Returns the address of a buffer containing the parsed string, which is stored as a counted string.

PARSE (*char — addr u*)

Parses the input stream to the first instance of *char*, returning the address and length of the parsed string.

WORD is the main workhorse of Forth's text interpreter. It fetches characters from the input stream (e.g., the terminal input buffer or a text file) — starting at the offset given by a variable called **>IN** — to a specified delimiter or the end of the input stream, whichever comes first, according to the following rules:

1. The input characters are placed in storage, conventionally at the next available location in the dictionary (whose address is returned by the word **HERE**), with the length

of the string in the first byte (i.e., a counted string).

2. The dictionary pointer is not modified.
3. The area where the characters are placed is not pre-initialized.
4. **WORD** returns the address of the counted string on the stack. This is a convenience for the words that conventionally follow it, such as **COUNT TYPE**.

The buffer in which **WORD** returns its parsed string is a transient area subject to frequent re-use. Therefore, when you use **WORD** to read a string from the input stream, you should finish working with the string or move it to another area promptly.

Try this
```
: TEST ( -- )   BL WORD COUNT TYPE ;
TEST ABC <cr> ABC ok
```

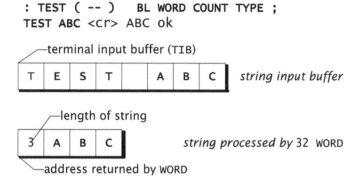

Try this
BL WORD ABC COUNT TYPE

What characters are typed out? Why?

PARSE differs from **WORD** in several important respects:

- **PARSE** doesn't skip leading delimiters, but **WORD** does.
- **PARSE** returns the address and length of the actual string, but **WORD** returns the address of a counted string.

One or the other is more useful, depending on the particular situation.

When you want to pick up all the remaining text on a line, the convention is to provide an argument of 0 or 1 to **WORD** or **PARSE**, as these numbers represent control codes you are unlikely to find in a normal text string, thus ensuring that the remainder of the line will be selected.

5.2.1 Problems

1. Define a word named **I'M** that accepts a string from the input stream and prints the string to the terminal:
   ```
   I'M FORTH <cr>   FORTH
   I'M NAME <cr>   NAME
   ```

2. Define a word named **MEET** that accepts a string from the input stream, prints **HI** and the string on the line below, then causes Forth's "ok" prompt to appear on the line below the string:

```
MEET FORTH <cr>
HI FORTH
ok
```

3. Define a space in **PAD** named **NAME**.
   Define a second space 40 bytes above **NAME** named **ADDR**.
   Define a third space 40 bytes above **ADDR** named **C/S**.

   Now define three words named **NAME?**, **ADDR?**, and **C/S?**, each used as follows:

   ```
   NAME? <cr> FORTH, Inc. <cr> ok
   ADDR? <cr> 5155 W.Rosecrans Ave. #1018 <cr> ok
   C/S? <cr> Hawthorne, CA <cr> ok
   ```

   Each word expects 40 characters from the keyboard and stores them at **NAME**, **ADDR**, and **C/S**, respectively.

   Now define a word named **?INFO** that prompts the user to enter the information for each field, and stores the data at **NAME**, **ADDR**, and **C/S**. It is used in the following way:

   ```
   ?INFO <cr>
   NAME? FORTH, Inc. <cr>
   ADDR? 6080 Center Drive<cr>
   C/S?  Los Angeles, CA <cr>
   ok
   ```

   Finally, define a word named **INFO** that is used in the following way:

   ```
   INFO <cr>
   FORTH, Inc.
   6080 Center Drive
   Los Angeles, CA   ok
   ```

   INFO prints the strings stored at **NAME**, **ADDR**, and **C/S**.

5.3 Compiling Strings

Compiled strings are used for labeling and display, for user prompts, error messages, and other purposes.

Glossary   The primary words for compiling strings are:

," $(-)$

Compiles a string terminated by a **"** as a counted string. Typically used to build a string data structure. ("comma-quote")

S" $(- addr\ u)$

Accepts a string from the input stream, either inside or outside a colon definition. When **S"** is used inside a colon definition, the string will be compiled such that, when the definition is executed, the string address and count will be on the stack.

When **s"** is used interpretively, *addr u* are returned. The string is terminated by a **"** (double-quote) character.

C"   (— addr)

Like **s"**, but returns the address of a counted string.

."   (—)

Used inside a colon definition, accepts from the input stream a string of characters terminated by a **"** (double-quote) and compiles it in the definition such that, when the definition is executed, the string will be typed out. ("dot-quote")

5.3.1 Compiling Strings Inside Definitions

s" compiles a string terminated by a **"** (double-quote) character. For example:

```
: .TEMP ( n -- )                    \ Display a temperature message
  68 > IF
    S" WARM "  ELSE  S" COOL "
  THEN TYPE ;
```

This will display the message WARM if the temperature value on the stack is greater than 68, or COOL otherwise.

C" is very similar to **s"**, but it compiles a counted string and returns its address as a single argument. Beyond that, it depends on the intended use whether the convenience of passing a single address outweighs the need to use **COUNT** to get the actual address and length.

The word **."** is used inside colon definitions only to compile a string that will be output when the word in which it appears is executed. For example:

```
: GREETING ( -- )   ." Hi there" ;
```

5.3.2 Strings Outside Definitions

s" and **C"** also may be executed interpretively, if you need temporary access to a string outside a colon definition. For example, **INCLUDED** loads a file, given the address and count of a string containing the filename. The syntax would be:

```
S" <filename>" INCLUDED
```

On many implementations, interpreted **s"** and **C"** use a single buffer to hold the string. Therefore, *successive uses of **s"** or **C"** may overwrite the buffer.*

Unlike **s"** and **C"** which provide temporary string access while interpreting, the word **,"** ("comma-quote") is use to *compile* a string into data space. This may be used after **CREATE** to compile a named string as in the following example:

```
CREATE NAME ," Acme Widgets, Inc."
: .NAME ( -- ) NAME COUNT TYPE ;
```

5.3.3 Special String Handling

SwiftForth from FORTH, Inc. includes similar string-defining words to support zero-terminated strings, strings with embedded control characters, and other similar structures. See the *SwiftForth Reference Manual* for details.

5.4 Terminal Control

Character-oriented display devices have various ways of managing common functions such as clear screen, new line, cursor positioning, etc. It would be cumbersome if all your display words had to be coded for each possible output device.

To solve this dilemma, Forth defines a number of convenient display management words to work on the *current output device*. Exactly how the current output device is selected is implementation-defined; on most FORTH, Inc. systems, each terminal task may have an output device associated with it, and versions of these words are available for each device supported. This is done using *vectored execution* (discussed in Section 7).

Glossary

CR (—)
Causes the cursor to move to column 0 of the next line on a display device, or to output the current line and advance to the next line on a printer.

PAGE (—)
Clears the display and moves the cursor to row 0, column 0. If the device is a printer, **PAGE** does a form feed.

AT-XY (x y —)
Moves the cursor to line *y*, column *x*.

GET-XY (— x y)
Returns the current column and row position of the cursor.

5.4.1 Problem: ?WAY Revisited

Convert the **?WAY** problem (Section 3.5.5) to move the cursor one position for each press of a direction key. The **HOME** function should position the cursor in the upper-left corner of the screen (position 0,0). This version should use **AT-XY** to move the cursor; all other characters must be sent to the display screen using **EMIT**.

5.5 Comparing Strings

Character-string comparisons operate on two separate character strings. This allows the two to be compared by using the collating sequence of the character set.

There are two relevant words, intended for quite different purposes:

- **SEARCH** is used to find a short string in a longer string, for example, in a text editor.
- **COMPARE** is used to compare two strings, for example, in a sort routine. It tells whether the strings match, and identifies the collating relationship between them.

Glossary

COMPARE
(*addr1 u1 addr2 u2 — n*)
Compares the first string to the second one and returns *n*. The strings are compared character-by-character, beginning at *addr1* and *addr2*, to the length of the shorter string or until a difference is found.

If *n* = 0, the strings are identical. If the strings are identical up to the length of the shorter string, *n* is -1 if *u1* is less than *u2*, and is +1 otherwise. If the strings are not identical up to the length of the shorter string, *n* is -1 if the first non-matching character in the string at *addr1* has a lesser numeric value than the corresponding character in the string at *addr2*, and is +1 otherwise.

SEARCH
(*addr1 u1 addr2 u2 — addr3 u3 flag*)
Searches in the string *addr1 u1* for a match to string *addr2 u2*. If a match is found, returns true with address *addr3* of the first matching character and the length *u3* of the remainder of the string. If no match is found, *addr3* = *addr1*, *u3* = *u1*, and *flag* is false. (If *u1* < *u2*, the search string will not be found.)

As an example of using **COMPARE**, you could compare a string whose address is returned by **NAME** with one temporarily stored at **PAD**, testing as follows:

```
PAD <length> NAME OVER COMPARE
```

Consider these two strings:

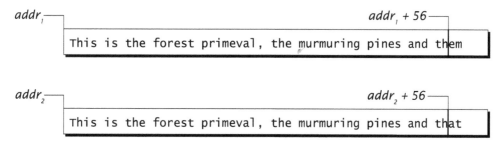

The following comparisons would yield these results:

Phrase	Result	Remarks
addr1 55 addr2 55 COMPARE	0	Strings are equal
addr1 56 addr2 56 COMPARE	1	String at *addr1* is later in collating sequence
addr1 55 addr2 56 COMPARE	-1	String at addr1 is shorter

As an example of **SEARCH**, consider these:

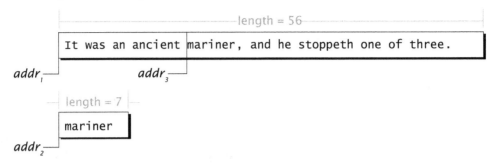

This phrase:

<addr1> **56** <addr2> **7 SEARCH**

...returns these results:

<addr3> **38 -1**

...because there is a match starting at *addr3* with 38 characters left in the first string.

5.6 Summary of String Commands

Input
ACCEPT
KEY, EKEY
KEY?, EKEY?

Output
TYPE
EMIT

Parse/Interpret
WORD
COUNT
PARSE
>IN

Move
MOVE
CMOVE
CMOVE>

Compare
COMPARE
SEARCH

Initialize
ERASE
BLANK
FILL

Compiling
,"
S"
C"

Miscellaneous
PAD
-TRAILING
CHAR and [CHAR]
BL
/STRING

Section 6: Number Conversion

6.1 Numeric Input

When you are testing an application using command-line input, you can take advantage of Forth's interactive nature. Thus, a hypothetical word **SCANS** whose function is to perform a user-specified number of scans should expect its parameter on the stack. Then to perform 100 scans, you could type:

100 SCANS

Such a usage is natural and convenient for the operator and requires no special programming to handle the input parameter.

In dialog boxes or menu-driven user interfaces, however, normal Forth syntax is inadequate. Forth provides several words to help you handle input numbers in a variety of circumstances. This section describes those methods.

First, let's review the basic algorithm for converting a string to a number:

1. Start with an "accumulator" (normally double-precision) on the stack, whose initial value is 0.
2. Take the most significant (leftmost) character in the string. Convert that digit to its binary equivalent. For decimal digits, this is as simple as subtracting the character code for the digit 0. Hex digits are more complicated; we'll get to them later.
3. Multiply the accumulator by the value in **BASE** (the current *radix*) and add the digit.
4. Repeat steps 2 and 3 until there are no more digits. The resulting integer is in the accumulator.

This limited summary leaves some open issues, such as what to do when the string is exhausted, or when you encounter a character that is not a digit. These issues are handled at various levels by the following input number conversion words.

Glossary

NUMBER   (*addr u — n / d*)
Attempts to convert string *addr u* into a binary number, using the radix (e.g., 10 for decimal, 16 for hex) in **BASE**. If valid punctuation (, . + - / :) is found, returns *d*; if there is no punctuation, returns *n*. If conversion fails due to a character that is neither a digit nor punctuation, an **ABORT** occurs.

NUMBER?   (*addr u — 0 / n 1 / d 2*)
Like **NUMBER**, but returns a flag on top of the stack describing the results:
0 = the string does not represent a number
1 = no punctuation in string, single number returned
2 = punctuation in string, double number returned.

>NUMBER   (*d1 addr1 u1 - d2 addr2 u2*)
Converts digits from the string *addr1 u1*, accumulating the digits in the number *d1*.

Conversion stops when any character that is not a legal digit (for the current radix value in **BASE**) is encountered, returning the result *d2* and the parameters *addr2 u2* for the remaining characters in the string.

>NUMBER is the standard, low-level input number conversion routine. If it encounters any non-numeric character during the conversion, it stops with a pointer to the character, rather than aborting. For this reason, **>NUMBER** is often used when a number is input by a program directly, without using the text interpreter. The initial address given to **>NUMBER** must point to the first digit of the string of numerals. The initial double-precision number is usually set to zero. **>NUMBER** uses the value in the user variable **BASE** to determine which radix should be used when converting numeric strings to binary.

After **>NUMBER** stops, the address in the second stack item is the address of the first non-numeric character encountered or, if the string was entirely converted, is the first character past the end of the string. The double-precision integer is the accumulated value of the digits converted thus far.

An example of the use of **>NUMBER** is:

```
: INPUT ( -- n )                \ Accept a single-length integer
   PAD 5 BLANK  PAD 5 ACCEPT     \ Get string
   >R  0. PAD R> >NUMBER         \ Convert double integer
   2DROP DROP ;                  \ single integer
```

This definition initializes a region of **PAD** to blanks and waits for up to five digits to store there. The **0.** provides an initial double-precision value, and **PAD R>** provides the address and actual count for **>NUMBER**. The **2DROP DROP** discards the address and count returned by **>NUMBER** and the high-order part of the converted number.

INPUT will not convert input strings with a leading minus sign, because a minus is not a numeric digit. If negative input is necessary, the above definition can be extended to first check whether the first character is a leading minus sign and, if it is, skip it, use **>NUMBER** to convert the remainder of the string, and negate the result at the end.

>NUMBER returns the address of the string's next byte, so **>NUMBER** may be called iteratively. The text interpreter's number-conversion routine calls **>NUMBER** in this way.

An application similar to this is parsing a packet of data received over a communications line, or from a tape record in which numeric fields are separated by an arbitrary delimiter such as //. To skip such items, or to skip fields that are not of interest, use **/STRING** to adjust the string's address and count to skip the appropriate number of bytes.

The word **NUMBER?** is a convenient high-level input number conversion routine. It performs number conversions from text to binary using **>NUMBER**. **NUMBER?** expects on the stack the address and length of the string that is to be converted. It will attempt to convert that string to binary and, if successful, will leave the result on the stack, below a flag that describes the result:

0 = conversion was unsuccessful (i.e., an illegal character was found),
1 = there was no punctuation and a single-precision integer follows, and

2 = there was punctuation and a double-length integer follows.

This allowance for the presence of punctuation characters was described in Section 2.4.2. Allowable punctuation characters include +, ., ,, /, :, and - anywhere except in the leading digit. If any punctuation was found, the number will be left as a double-precision integer, and the number of digits to the right of the rightmost punctuation will be found in the variable **DPL**. If there was no punctuation, *what would have been the high-order part of a double number* is left in the variable **NH**. This lets you convert numbers such as 99999 without punctuation on a 16-bit implementation.

A side-effect of that fact that **NUMBER?** will accept punctuation character is the requirement that the numeric string must be terminated by a space. To facilitate this, SwiftForth ensures that at least one trailing space is at the end of any buffer returned by **ACCEPT**.[12]

The highest-level input number conversion word in FORTH, Inc. systems is **NUMBER**. **NUMBER** calls **NUMBER?**, and additionally tests the flag returned by **NUMBER?**. If the conversion fails due to illegal characters, an abort will occur with an error message echoing the string followed by a question mark ("?").

Try this

```
PAD 10 ACCEPT <cr> 12345
```

...returns the actual length of the string that received into **PAD**.

```
PAD SWAP NUMBER
```

...returns 12345 on the stack).

Try some punctuated numbers.

As an example use of **NUMBER** we can define the word **TRY**:

```
: TRY ( -- )    ." Type a number: "  PAD 10 ACCEPT
    PAD SWAP NUMBER   DPL @ DUP 0< IF
        ." Single, = " DROP .
    ELSE ." Double, " . ." Places, = "
    D. THEN ;
```

NUMBER or **NUMBER?** may be used to convert a string from another location (e.g., a string that has not been fetched by use of **WORD** or **ACCEPT**). If it is not feasible to guarantee the trailing space, you may prefer to move the string to **PAD**, as shown below, or use **>NUMBER** and decide what to do when it encounters a non-digit.

Assume a string at *addr u*:

```
: CONVERT-IT ( addr u -- n | d )   >R\ Save len
    PAD R@ 1+ BLANK   PAD R@ MOVE   \ Move string
    PAD R> NUMBER ;                 \ Convert
```

---

12. The trailing space is not included in the count returned by **ACCEPT**.

6.1.1 Problem: IP Address

Write a word GET-IP that will accept from the input stream a number of the form
nnn.nnn.nnn.nnn and will break it into four numeric segments that are left in four
consecutive bytes of a buffer called PARTS. Assume that any individual part may
contain one to three digits, and no individual part will be greater than 255.

6.2 Numeric Output

Forth contains a set words that allow numeric quantities to be output through use
of a *pictured* output control. These words allow specification of all aspects of the
numeric output format.

6.2.1 Basic Principles

In Forth, the description of these words starts at the low-order portion of the field
and continues to the high-order portion. Although this is the reverse of the method
apparently used in other languages, it is the internal conversion process in all languages. Recall that BASE contains the current conversion radix. The basic algorithm
is the exact converse of the input conversion algorithm, as follows:

1. Start with an unsigned, double-length number. If you'll be treating this as a signed
   number, you must first save the sign information (later we'll see how).
2. Divide the number by the value in BASE, getting a quotient and remainder. The
   remainder is the value of a single digit; the first time, it's the low-order (rightmost)
   digit, moving successively toward higher-order digits.
3. Convert the remainder to a printable character by adding the character code for 0
   and appending the resulting character to a string being built from right to left.
4. Continue for as many digits you want, or until the quotient reaches zero (depending
   on your choice of words).
5. Discard the quotient, and return the address and length of the string.

   These steps are performed by a set of words described in Section 6.2.2, which provides complete control over the process and the appearance of the resulting string.
   These words convert numbers on the stack into printable character strings con-
   forming to the format requirements. The converted string can be displayed using
   TYPE or can be used in some other way.

   In many systems, strings are built in an area in memory that immediately follows
   the end of the dictionary (the address left by HERE). This area is large enough to
   accommodate at least 32 characters of output (64 characters on 32-bit machines).
   All the standard numeric output words use the same region. As a result, these
   words may not be executed while a pictured numeric output conversion is in process (e.g., during debugging). Furthermore, you must not make new definitions
   during the pictured numeric conversion process, as this would overwrite the area in
   which the string is being generated.

6.2.2 High-level Numeric Output Words

Several standard words allow you to display single- or double-precision, signed or unsigned numbers in various formats. All of them remove their arguments from the stack. To preserve a number you are about to display, use DUP first. Each display word produces an output string that consists of the following characters:

1. If the number is negative, a leading minus sign.
2. The absolute value of the number, with leading zeroes suppressed. (The number zero results in a single zero in the output.)
3. In some cases, a trailing blank.

Glossary   The standard numeric output words are:

. $(n -)$
Displays *n* as a signed, single-precision integer followed by one space.

.R $(n1 +n2 -)$
Displays the signed, single-precision integer *n1* with leading spaces, to fill a field of width *+n2*, right-justified. The width of the printed string that would be output by . is used to determine the number of leading blanks. No trailing blanks are printed. If the magnitude of the number to be printed prevents printing within the number of spaces specified, all digits are displayed with no leading spaces in a field as wide as necessary.

? $(addr -)$
Displays the contents of *addr*. Equivalent to the phrase: @ .

D. $(d -)$
Displays *d* as a signed, double-precision integer.

D.R $(d +n -)$
Displays *d* as a signed, double-precision integer in a field of width *+n*, as for .R.

U. $(u -)$
Displays *u* as an unsigned, single-precision integer followed by one space.

U.R $(u +n -)$
Unsigned version of .R. Displays *u* with leading spaces to fill a field of width *+n*, right-justified.

6.2.3 Pictured Numeric Output Words

These words provide control over conversion of binary numbers into digits. Conversion is initiated by <#. Throughout the process, the number being operated on is on the stack, repeatedly divided by the number radix (in BASE) as digits are converted. The remaining number is discarded by #> at the end of the process.

Glossary

<#   (—)

Begins formatted output of an unsigned double-precision integer.

(ud1 — ud2)

Prepends the next digit to the string. Must be used between **<#** and **#>** (though not necessarily in the same definition). The first digit added is the lowest-order digit (units), the next digit is the tens digit, etc. Each time **#** is used, a digit is generated, regardless of whether or not it is a significant digit.

#S   (ud1 — ud2)

Converts digits repetitively until all significant digits have been converted, at which point conversion is complete. Must be used between **<#** and **#>**. **#S** always results in at least one output character, even if the number to be converted is a zero.

SIGN   (n —)

Inserts a minus sign at the current position in the output string if *n* is negative. The magnitude of *n* is irrelevant, only its sign is of interest. In order for the sign to appear at the left of the number (the usual place), **SIGN** must be called *after* all digits have been converted.

HOLD   (char —)

Inserts a character at the current position in the output string. The character code to be inserted must be on the stack.

#>   (ud — addr u)

Completes the conversion process after all digits have been converted. This word discards the (presumably exhausted) double-precision number, and pushes onto the stack the address of the output string and its count.

Consider one possible definition of the standard Forth word . ("dot"):

```
: . ( n -- )                \ Display n
  DUP ABS 0                 \ Prepare
  <# #S  ROT SIGN #>        \ Convert string
  TYPE SPACE ;              \ Output string
```

DUP ABS leaves two numbers on the stack: the absolute value of the number on top of the number itself, which is now useful only for its sign. 0 adds a cell on top of the stack, so that the 0 cell and the **ABS** cell form a double-precision integer to be used by the **<#** ... **#>** routines.

To print a signed, double-precision integer with the low-order three digits always appearing, regardless of their value, you could use the following definition:

```
: NNN ( d -- )              \ Display d, with at least 3 digits
  SWAP OVER DABS            \ Prepare
  <# # # #S  ROT SIGN #>    \ Convert string
  TYPE SPACE ;              \ Output string
```

The phrase **SWAP OVER DABS** puts the signed value beneath the absolute value of the number to be printed, for use by the word **SIGN**. The sequence **# #** converts the low-order two digits, regardless of value. The word **#S** converts the remaining digits and always results in at least one character of output, even if the value is zero.

From the time the initialization word **<#** executes until the terminating **#>** executes, the number being converted is on the stack. It's possible to use the stack for intermediate results during formatted processing, but anything put on the stack must be removed before any subsequent picture editing or fill characters may be processed.

6.2.4 Using Pictured Fill Characters

In addition to pictured numeric output, it is possible to introduce fill characters (or punctuation) into the output string through the use of **HOLD**. When words such as the examples in this section are used, the appropriate character is entered into the output string at the current position. Using words such as these improves the readability of your code, and may also save space (if they are re-used several times).

HOLD requires as a parameter the character code to be inserted. Thus,

```
CHAR - HOLD
```

...inserts the minus character the output string.

```
: '.' ( -- )   [CHAR] . HOLD ;
```

The word **'.'** produces a decimal point at the current position in the pictured numeric output. To illustrate, the word **.$** below will print double-precision integers as signed amounts with two decimal places:

```
: .$ ( d -- )              \ Display a number as dollars & cents
    SWAP OVER DABS         \ Prepare
    <# # # '.' #S ROT SIGN #>   \ Convert string
    TYPE  SPACE ;          \ Display
```

If fill characters are likely to be used in several definitions, you may wish to add commands similar to **'.'** above.

6.2.5 Processing Special Characters

The pictured output capabilities described in the preceding two sections are sufficient to handle most output requirements. Special cases, however, such as the introduction of commas in a number or the floating of a character (such as a currency symbol), require special processing. In order to perform certain of these operations, it is necessary to refer to the unconverted portion of a number being printed.

This unconverted portion is a number equivalent to the original number divided by 10 (or the current radix) for each numeric digit already generated. For example, if the initial number is 123, the intermediate number is 12 (following the conversion of the first digit) and 1 (following conversion of the second digit).

The value of this number may be tested, and logical decisions may be based on its value. To illustrate, consider the following definitions. The word **D.ENG** prints a double-precision integer in engineering format:

```
: ',' ( -- )    [CHAR] , HOLD ;

: (D.ENG) ( d -- addr u)   SWAP OVER DABS  <#
   BEGIN  3 0 DO
          #  2DUP D0= IF  LEAVE  THEN    LOOP
      2DUP D0= NOT WHILE  ',' REPEAT
   ROT SIGN #> ;

: D.ENG ( d -- )   (D.ENG) TYPE  SPACE ;
```

Using techniques similar to those above, you can do almost any kind of numeric output formatting in Forth.

6.2.6 Problems

1. Define a word named .SSN that accepts a double-precision number from the stack and prints it in the form of a social security number.

   .SSN is used in the following way:

   111223333. .SSN 111-22-3333

2. Define a word .PH to accept a single-precision and a double-precision number from the stack and prints them in the form of an area code and a telephone number.

   .PH is used in the following way:

   310 491.3356 .PH (310) 491-3356

3. Define a word named N.2 that accepts a signed, single-precision number from the stack and prints it with two digits to the right of the decimal point, with a preceding minus sign if the number is negative.

   N.2 is used in the following way:

   -12345 N.2 -123.45

4. Define a word named DF. that accepts two numbers from the stack. The second number on the stack is a double-precision number and at the top of the stack is a single-precision number. The double-precision number is to be printed, together with a preceding minus sign if the number is negative, with the single-cell number representing the number of digits to the right of the decimal point.

   DF. is used in the following way:

   12345. 3 DF. 12.345
   -12345. 1 DF. -1234.5

5. The commands BASE ? yield 10 regardless of the base in which Forth is operating at the time. Define a word named ?BASE that will print the base in decimal without permanently altering it.

   ?BASE is used in the following way:[13]

```
DECIMAL ?BASE 10
HEX ?BASE 16
OCTAL ?BASE 8
2 BASE ! ?BASE 2
```

6.3 Summary of Number Conversion Words

Input	Formatting	Output
>NUMBER	<#	.
NUMBER	#>	.R
NUMBER?	#	?
BASE	#S	D.
DPL	HOLD	U.
NH	SIGN	D.R
		U.R

---

13. If OCTAL is not defined on your system, use **8 BASE** ! instead.

Section 7: Vectored Execution

7.1 Basic Principles

Vectored execution enables us to indirectly execute, or change the operation of, a word after it has been defined. We do this by specifying a word's execution token (or *xt*) and then executing it. An *xt* is commonly kept in a variable for easy access.

An execution token is a special kind of pointer to a Forth word that is returned by a phrase such as:

```
' <name>
```

...or...

```
['] <name>
```

...inside a definition.

The execution token of *name* may then be passed to the word **EXECUTE**, which will execute it. On some implementations, an *xt* is an address; on others, it is a special kind of pointer, table index, or offset.

The word **EXECUTE** expects on the stack the execution token of a definition.

Glossary

Note that where two stack pictures are given below, the first is the *compile-time* stack effect and the second is the *run-time* stack effect.

'

$$(- xt)$$

Parses the next word from the input stream and returns its *xt*. Aborts if the word isn't found in the dictionary. Pronounced "tick."

[']

$$(-)$$
$$(- xt)$$

Used inside a colon definition. Parses the next word in the input stream at compile time, and compiles its *xt* as a literal. Aborts if the word isn't found in the dictionary.

EXECUTE

$$(xt -)$$

Executes the word whose *xt* is on the stack. Arguments to the word to be executed (if any) must be on the stack below the *xt*.

Try this

```
VARIABLE MEAL

: 7AM  ( -- )    CR ." Breakfast " ;
: 12PM ( -- )  CR ." Lunch " ;
: 6PM  ( -- )    CR ." Supper " ;

: MORNING ( -- )    ['] 7AM  MEAL ! ;
: NOON ( -- )    ['] 12PM MEAL ! ;
: NIGHT ( -- )    ['] 6PM  MEAL ! ;
```

```
: SERVE ( -- )    MEAL @ EXECUTE ;
```

If the user types:

MORNING SERVE

...the computer will type:

Breakfast

Typing:

NIGHT SERVE

...will produce:

Supper

Note that other actions can occur between **NIGHT** and **SERVE** without changing this behavior. Further, **SERVE** may be executed as many times as needed without its action changing: only typing **MORNING, NOON,** or **NIGHT** will change the action of **SERVE**.

The word **[']** searches the dictionary for the next word in the definition. If it finds the word, it compiles the word's execution token into the dictionary as a literal. **[']** must be used inside a colon definition.

To get the *xt* of a word from the input stream, use **'** ("tick"). It gets the next word from the input stream, looks it up in the dictionary, and returns its *xt* on the stack.

The phrase **@ EXECUTE** is so common that FORTH, Inc. systems provide the word **@EXECUTE** to save space and CPU time. The behavior of **@EXECUTE** is the same as the phrase **@ EXECUTE,** with the addition of a check on the contents of the address supplied. If it contains zero (which is not a valid *xt*), **@EXECUTE** will simply return to the calling definition without performing any operation.[14] This means that execution vectors may not require special initialization.

All members of a set of words to be vectored through a single execution vector must share the same stack effect. That is, they must all require or leave the same number of items on the stack.

The word **DEFER** provides a convenient means of managing a single execution vector. The word **IS** provides a method to put another word's *xt* into the vector.

The syntax is:

```
DEFER <name>
<xt> IS <name>
```

DEFER defines *name* and makes it an execution vector. The execution token of the word to be executed is stored into the data area of *name* by the word **IS**. An error will occur if *name* is executed before it has been initialized by **IS**.

DEFER lets you change the execution of previously defined commands by creating a slot that can be loaded with different behaviors at different times.

---

14. Ignoring a zero *xt* is appropriate only in cases where there are no stack arguments.

Try this   The "mealtime" example above could be defined this way using **DEFER** and **IS**:

```
DEFER SERVE

: 7AM ( -- )    CR ." Breakfast " ;
: 12PM ( -- )   CR ." Lunch " ;
: 6PM ( -- )    CR ." Supper " ;

: MORNING ( -- )    ['] 7AM  IS SERVE ;
: NOON  ( -- )      ['] 12PM IS SERVE ;
: NIGHT ( -- )      ['] 6PM  IS SERVE ;
```

The usage is identical. For example:

```
MORNING SERVE
```

...but there was no need to define **SERVE** as a separate definition, because invoking a word defined by **DEFER** automatically causes the *xt* it contains to be executed.

7.2 Execution Vectors

An execution vector is an array, each cell of which holds the *xt* of a previously defined word. Here is an exercise in how to compute an offset into such an array.

We will define a set of words, each of which prints a greeting in some language (Hello, Bonjour, etc.). We'll then build a table containing the *xt* of each greeting. Finally, we'll define a word named **GREETING** which, given a named element on the stack, calculates the address of that element, fetches the content and executes it.

Here's how this code might look:

```
: ENGLISH-GREETING ( -- )  ." Hello, my friend" ;
: FRENCH-GREETING ( -- )   ." Bonjour, mon ami" ;
: GERMAN-GREETING ( -- )   ." Guten Tag, mein Freund" ;
: AUSSIE-GREETING ( -- )   ." G'day, mate ;

CREATE GREETINGS
    ' ENGLISH-GREETING ,       \ 0
    ' FRENCH-GREETING ,        \ 1
    ' GERMAN-GREETING ,        \ 2
    ' AUSSIE-GREETING ,        \ 3
0 CONSTANT ENGLISH
1 CONSTANT FRENCH
2 CONSTANT GERMAN
3 CONSTANT AUSSIE

: GREETING ( n -- )              \ Display the selected greeting
    0 MAX  3 MIN                 \ Clip n to legal values
    CELLS GREETINGS + @EXECUTE ; \ Display greeting
```

This strategy is most valuable when the selection mechanism is inherently numeric, such as associating behaviors with a set of function keys or push buttons. In such a case, you would convert the code returned by the key or button pad to an index into your array.

If the values aren't dense, you can leave some zeroes in the array; remember that **@EXECUTE** will treat them as no-ops. It's also convenient when a selection is made every time, whereas **DEFER** is preferable for a "mode" that is persistent.

Both vector tables and **DEFER** words are useful when you can't define all the possible behaviors before the mechanism that will invoke them.

7.2.1 Problem: ?WAY Revisited Again

Convert your **?WAY** problem (Section 3.5.5 and Section 5.4.1) to use vectored execution, using your input key (I, J, K, L, M) as a selector.

7.3 Button Tables

Most uses of vectored execution are for implementing a variable function as described in the previous section. The ability to generate and manage a table of execution tokens is also extremely useful for such purposes as managing a function-button pad, function menu on a graphics tablet, etc. This section will outline another simple button-response application that may serve as a model for similar situations.

Vectored execution is very useful for push button control panels; all the good qualities — readability, testability, modularity — are working together here.

Let us assume that the word **BUTTON** has been defined to wait until a button is pressed and then to return the button number (0–15) of the button (the actual definition of **BUTTON** would depend on the computer and interface). Now consider the following:

```
16 CELLS BUFFER: BUTTONS

: IGNORE ;
' IGNORE BUTTONS ! BUTTONS DUP CELL+ 15 CELLS CMOVE
```

These lines create a table with one cell for each button, and initialize all positions to contain the address of an empty definition (effectively ignoring any undefined button). The move and replication of the **IGNORE** address must be done with a **CMOVE** instead of a **MOVE**, because **CMOVE** moves bytes from lower to higher overlapping locations, achieving the replication of the address.

Next, we'll define a word that will insert an *xt* into a specified cell of the table:

```
: B: ( n -- )    '  SWAP CELLS BUTTONS + ! ;
```

Now we can create definitions and attach them to certain buttons by using **B:** with the button number as a parameter. Each such definition will have a name, to allow it to be tested independently of the button pad. For example,

```
: ESCAPE    1 ABORT" ? " ;
```

```
0 B: ESCAPE
```

...defines Button 0 to be an "escape" button, using the standard Forth abort-with-message word **ABORT"** (discussed in Section 8.5.1). This strategy allows you to define buttons in different parts of the application, whereas the previous method requires all table entries to be defined before you define the **GREETING** handler.

All that remains is to define a routine to monitor the button pad and to handle responses:

```
: MONITOR ( -- )                        \ Respond to button presses
    BEGIN  BUTTON CELLS
        BUTTONS + @EXECUTE
    AGAIN ;
```

Typing **MONITOR** will place the terminal task in an infinite loop that responds to buttons. Button 0 will cause an abort and return control to the terminal.

In practice, **MONITOR** may very likely be executed by a background task (on systems that support multitasking). In this case, you may need techniques other than **ABORT"** (which requires some kind of output device) for halting. Background tasks, and multitasking in general, are discussed in Section 10.

Section 8: Advanced Concepts

8.1 Dictionary

The dictionary is a linked list of Forth words. Before a word can be executed, it must be found in the dictionary. This is done by sequentially searching the dictionary, starting with the latest definition and searching backward through earlier ones. To speed these searches, the dictionary may be organized into multiple threads; the particular thread a word will be in depends upon a hash value computed from its name and the word list in which it is defined. Word lists are discussed in more detail beginning in Section 8.2.

8.1.1 Structure of a Word

Each word in the dictionary shares the same basic structure as shown in Figure 13.

Figure 13. Dictionary structure

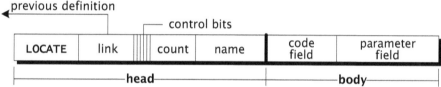

The head of a Forth word consists of a link field that points to the previous definition in the dictionary, a length byte that holds the actual number of characters in the name field, and other fields.

The longest possible name in SwiftForth is 254 characters (and 32 in many other systems), so a byte is enough to express the count of characters in the word's name.

The head also has *control bits* used to determine how the word will be handled. One is called the *smudge bit*. This bit is set by : (colon) to render the word invisible to dictionary searches, and is reset by ; (semicolon) to make the word visible again. This prevents inadvertent recursion caused by a word compiling a reference to itself, and also prevents calling a word that did not finish compiling due to an error. Another control bit is the *precedence bit*. When it is set, the word will be executed by the compiler when encountered inside a colon definition (instead of being compiled, like normal words). Words that behave in this manner are called *immediate words* (because they execute immediately, rather than later). Examples include DO, LOOP, IF, ELSE, THEN, and other flow-of-control structure words.

The rest of a dictionary entry consists of the word's code field and parameter field. The code field identifies a word's run-time code. The parameter field follows the code field, and varies in length depending upon the type of word. The content of the code and parameter fields depends upon the strategy used to implement Forth on this platform. For example, in some cases you might find the parameter field of a colon definition contains pointers to previously defined words; in other cases, references to other words are subroutine calls. Some systems embed code in place.

In SwiftForth, data objects have both a code field and a parameter field (the latter containing the data or a pointer to the data), but colon definitions only have executable code fields. In the SwiftX cross-compiler, the target system's dictionary is split: the heads remain in the host, and only executable code and data fields reside in the target. An optional add-on to SwiftX supports a target-resident interpreter, in which case some or all target words may also have heads.

The general relationship between dictionary entries is shown in Figure 14.

Figure 14. Linked dictionary entries

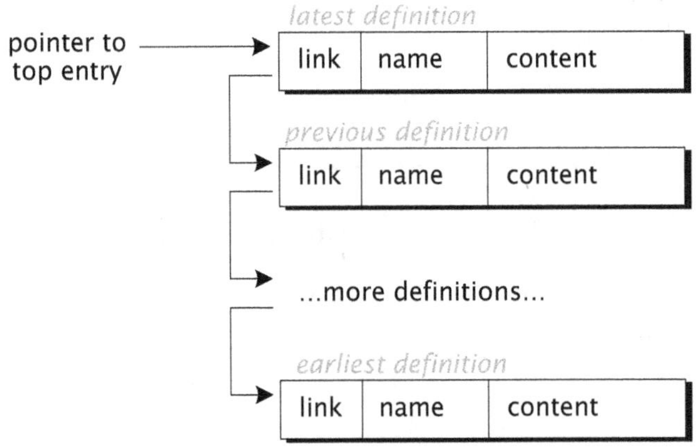

8.1.2 How Words are Created

A word in Forth is defined when its entry is created in the dictionary. This process involves the following steps:

1. The next space-delimited string is parsed from the input stream. This will be the word's name.
2. The definition is linked to the previous definition in the chain controlling the dictionary search.
3. A pointer is set to the head of the chain containing the new word.
4. Space is allotted for the new word's name.
5. The code field is set to point to the instance behavior code for **CREATE**.

If there is not enough memory remaining to create the new entry in the dictionary, some implementation-specific action will occur. This may be as simple as aborting with an error message ("Dictionary full") or something more complex, like requesting more memory from the host operating system.

In Section 8.6, we'll see how you can define new classes of words.

8.1.3 Managing the Dictionary

If you have definitions you no longer need and you would like to recover the space they use, you can use the word EMPTY.

EMPTY resets your working dictionary back to its prior state. This has the effect of forgetting, or clearing, all the definitions you have entered into the dictionary. This is frequently useful when you are repeatedly loading a large application to test.

Note that the kernel and the system dictionary are not affected by EMPTY (the system dictionary contains words loaded when the system boots).

You may wish to subdivide a large application during development so you can repeatedly reload the portion under test while leaving more stable, underlying support functions untouched. This may be done with overlays. Because Forth compilers are so fast, Forth systems rarely support or require run-time overlays of pre-compiled code; the kind of overlays we're speaking of here are groups of functions compiled from source.

Overlays are facilitated by the word MARKER. The phrase MARKER <name> creates a dictionary entry for *name*. When *name* is executed, it will discard the definition *name* and all words defined after *name*. The dictionary pointer will be reset to the last definition in the vocabulary before *name*. Other system-dependent actions may be taken as well, such as restoration of interrupt vectors (see your system documentation).

MARKER has two uses:

- To discard only some of your definitions. For example, when testing, you may wish to reload only the last file, not your entire application.
- To create additional levels of overlays.

Suppose your application includes an overlay called GRAPHICS. After GRAPHICS is loaded, you want to be able to load one of two additional overlays, called COLOR and B&W, thus creating a second level of overlay. Here is the procedure to follow:

1. Define a marker as the final definition of GRAPHICS, using any word you want as a dictionary marker. For example:

   ```
   MARKER OVERLAY
   ```

   A good place for this definition would be at the end of the graphics load file.

2. Execute OVERLAY to discard any definitions added since it was defined, and then redefine it (because it forgets itself) on the first line of the load file of each level-two overlay. The following example might be the first line of an overlay load file Color.f:

   ```
   OVERLAY    MARKER OVERLAY
   ```

   Thus, when you execute the phrase:

   ```
   INCLUDE COLOR.F
   ```

   ...the system will forget any definitions compiled after the original definition of OVERLAY (the one defined in Step 1 above), and will restore the marker definition of

OVERLAY in the event you want to either discard the color definitions and reload them, or load an alternate level-two set of definitions, such as B&W.

Use different names for your markers to create any number of overlay levels.

SwiftForth includes a more complex overlay support facility capable of saving and restoring elements of the program's state in addition to the dictionary, such as default values for DEFER words, Windows settings, and other environmental issues. This is documented in the *SwiftForth Reference Manual*.

8.2 Search Orders and Word Lists

Now that we have discussed the dictionary in more detail, you might be wondering how words like IF work. In many systems, there are two versions of IF: one for conditionals in high-level Forth, and another for analogous structures in the assembler. They are distinguishable from each other in the dictionary because they are defined in different word lists.

Space in the dictionary is allotted sequentially, with new entries having higher addresses than older entries. However, when the text interpreter searches the dictionary, it follows a linked list or chain of definitions, starting with the most recent definition in that chain. There may be several such linked lists intermingled in the memory space occupied by the dictionary. Such a linked list is called a *word list*. Multiple word lists may be searched sequentially. If searching the first fails to yield a match, a second may be searched, and so on through a specified sequence. A defined sequence of word lists is called a *search order*.

At least two standard word lists are provided by most Forth implementations: FORTH and ASSEMBLER. These hold regular Forth words and assembler definitions, respectively. You may also define your own word lists.

8.2.1 Managing Word Lists

A Forth system usually contains several built-in word lists. To get a list of all the words in a word list, put the word list in the search order by typing its name followed by WORDS. For example:

FORTH WORDS

On SwiftForth, you can also use the Words toolbar button. SwiftForth's Words dialog box includes a pull-down list of all the word lists available for display.

Each of the word lists in the system has a unique numeric identifier, called a *wid*, or word list identifier. Here are some words for manipulating word lists:

Glossary

<word-list-name>   (—)
Makes the specified word list the first one in the search order, replacing the one

that was previously first.

ALSO   (—)

Duplicates the first word list in the search order, increasing the number of word lists in the search order by one. **ALSO** is commonly followed by the name of a search order, which replaces the top word list, so the effect is the new word list is added to the previous list.

CONTEXT   (— *addr*)

Returns the address of a user variable that determines the dictionary search order.

CURRENT   (— *addr*)

Returns the address of a user variable specifying the word list in which new word definitions will be appended.

DEFINITIONS   (—)

The compilation word list (the one specified by **CURRENT**) is changed to be the same as the first word list in the search order.

ONLY   (—)

Reduces the search order to contain only the minimum word lists, usually **FORTH**.

ORDER   (—)

Displays the word list names forming the search order in their present search order sequence. Also displays the word list into which new definitions will be placed (the **CURRENT** word list).

PREVIOUS   (—)

Removes the first word list (the one in the **CONTEXT** position) from the search order. This may be used to undo the effect of an **ALSO**.

VOCABULARY <name>   (—)

A dictionary entry for *name* is created which specifies a new ordered list of word definitions. Subsequent execution of *name* replaces the first word list in the search order with *name*.

WORDS   (—)

Displays the names of all the words of the first word list in the search order.

8.2.2 Word List Access

Word lists may be searched individually or in groups in a specified order. Each word list may have multiple chains to speed dictionary searches. The user variable **CONTEXT** contains the sequence of word lists to be searched. The contents of **CONTEXT** may be changed by naming the desired word list, for example:

    ASSEMBLER

Hereafter, future searches will begin with the **ASSEMBLER** word list.

You may display the current search order by typing **ORDER**.

New definitions are compiled into the word list indicated by the value of **CURRENT**. The word list specified by **CURRENT** may be changed by using the name of the desired word list, followed by the word **DEFINITIONS**, which sets **CURRENT** equal to **CONTEXT**. So, to make Forth search the **ASSEMBLER** word list and add new definitions to it, use:

```
ASSEMBLER DEFINITIONS
```

The word **ASSEMBLER** sets **CONTEXT** to that word list. **DEFINITIONS** then sets **CURRENT** equal to **CONTEXT**. All new words will be compiled into the **ASSEMBLER** word list until **CURRENT** is explicitly changed by a similar statement.

The default word list for both **CONTEXT** and **CURRENT** is **FORTH**. This is set whenever the system is powered up or the dictionary is emptied.

8.2.3 Sealed Word Lists

The word list mechanism offers the potential for an exceptionally powerful security technique. You can implement this by setting up a special application word list consisting of a limited number of commands guaranteed to be safe for users. You then ensure no application word can change **CONTEXT**, and **CONTEXT** is set so the text interpreter will only search the application word list.

This has the effect of sealing a task into its limited word list and rendering all other words unfindable. Here is how a sealed word list is constructed:

1. Define a new word list for the findable words. For example:
   ```
   VOCABULARY APPLICATION
   ```
2. Place all user definitions in the **APPLICATION** word list by declaring:
   ```
   APPLICATION DEFINITIONS
   ```

Note that, when definitions for the **APPLICATION** word list are being compiled, **FORTH** must be included in the search order:

```
ONLY FORTH ALSO APPLICATION DEFINITIONS
```

3. Define **SEALED** like this:
   ```
   : SEALED ( -- ) ONLY APPLICATION ;
   ```

When **SEALED** is executed, only definitions in **APPLICATION** can be accessed. **SEALED** might be executed at the end of the application load file, and only when the application has been completely tested.

CONTEXT cannot be changed by a reference to its name, because the variable **CONTEXT** is defined in the **FORTH** word list that is sealed from search, as are all words that would enable a knowledgeable user to change **CONTEXT**.

8.3 Text Interpreter

The words you type are processed by a text interpreter. Although its basic functionality is the same in all Forth systems, factoring and implementation details vary. A general diagram of the process is shown in Figure 15.

Functions for processing the input stream, searching the dictionary, and attempting number conversion are shared by the compiler. The difference in behavior depends upon a variable called **STATE**. If **STATE** is zero, a word found in the dictionary will be executed or a successfully converted number will be pushed on the stack. If **STATE** is non-zero, a word will be compiled (unless it is **IMMEDIATE**, as described in Section 8.4) or a number will be compiled as a literal.

The text interpreter character pointer **>IN** points to the character immediately following the last word that was interpreted from the input stream. This is a relative pointer indicating (in characters) how far into the input stream the interpreter has gone.

There are three ways of leaving the interpreter:

1. By successfully reaching the end of the input stream, in which case Forth says ok.
2. By aborting on a stack underflow (e.g., if a word needed an argument that was not there).
3. By aborting if the string was not a valid word or valid number.

Either of the last two exit conditions will generate an error message.

8.3.1 Interpreting Text From the Keyboard

The terminal is the default source for the input stream passed to **INTERPRET**. The interaction between your typing and the text interpreter's processing of the commands you type is controlled by the word **QUIT**.

QUIT is the outer loop of an interactive Forth (e.g., in SwiftForth's command window). This means that all you must do to use Forth is start up the system and you will be executing the Forth word QUIT.

Figure 15. The text interpreter.

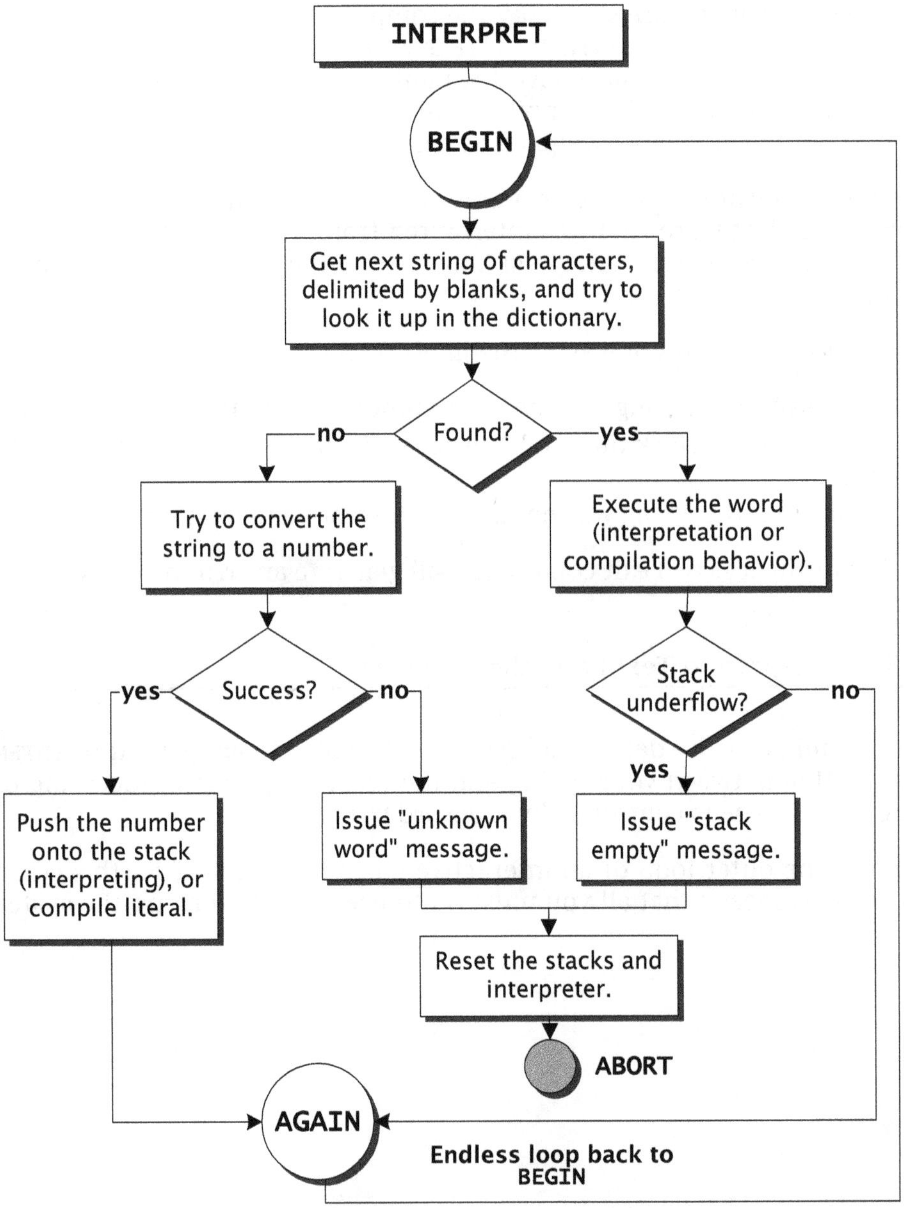

QUIT (see Figure 16) has a very simple operating procedure:

1. QUIT queries the terminal for a Forth command line. Any input it finds is put in the *Terminal Input Buffer* (TIB), which will accept a line of characters for processing. The actual number of characters received is contained in the variable #TIB. The text interpreter begins processing the input stream upon receipt of a line-terminating character.

2. Upon receiving the end-of-line character, QUIT calls INTERPRET to attempt to execute each word in sequence.

3. Upon successfully finishing the line in **INTERPRET**, **QUIT** displays the message "ok."

Figure 16. Simplified QUIT flowchart

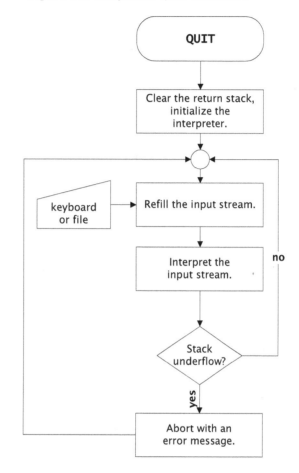

Try this   Type the Enter (or Return) key over and over again. Try typing the word **QUIT**.

Note: The "ok" message does not mean that what you executed was okay, it just means that Forth was able to complete whatever tasks you assigned it and is ready for a new command line to be entered.

8.3.2 Interpreting Text From Other Sources

Standard Forth defines a total of four potential sources for the input stream that is passed to the text interpreter:

1. The terminal input buffer (as acquired by **QUIT**), discussed in Section 8.3.1.
2. Disk blocks, or 1024-byte chunks of disk, typically supported by native Forth systems and classical Forth implementations. Blocks are discussed in detail in *Forth Programmer's Handbook*.

3. Text files, as discussed in Section 9.1.4.

4. An arbitrary string passed to the word **EVALUATE**.

The *current input stream* is defined by the word **SOURCE-ID** and the variable **BLK**, as follows:

- If **SOURCE-ID** returns zero and **BLK** contains zero, the source is the Terminal Input Buffer (**TIB**) and its length is in **#TIB**.

- If **BLK** contains non-zero, its value is assumed to be the number of a disk block to interpret, and **SOURCE-ID** is ignored.

- If **BLK** contains zero and **SOURCE-ID** returns -1, the input stream is a text string whose address and length were passed to **EVALUATE**.

- If **BLK** contains zero and **SOURCE-ID** returns a non-zero value (other than -1 as noted above), the value returned by **SOURCE-ID** is assumed to be the *fileid* of a text file to interpret line-by-line by using **INCLUDE-FILE** (or higher-level **INCLUDE** words) or by reading successive lines into a buffer using **REFILL**.

The state of the current input stream also includes **>IN**, which starts with a value of zero when a new input source is being processed and progresses with each interpreted word. There also may be implementation-specific parameters.

It is possible to nest input streams. For example, if you type:

```
INCLUDE <filename>
```

...the current state of the terminal input buffer will be saved during the processing of *filename* and, if that file also contains **INCLUDE** commands, they will nest as well.

The word **SOURCE** returns the address and length of the current input stream, whatever it may be. If the input stream is coming from disk, the address is that of text that has been read from disk and is available for processing.

Glossary   Following is a summary of the words used for managing the input stream.

BLK   (— *addr*)
Contains zero or the block number of a block being interpreted.

SOURCE-ID   (— *addr*)
Contains zero, -1, or the *fileid* of a file being interpreted.

>IN   (— *addr*)
Contains a relative pointer to the next character in the current input stream to be interpreted.

SOURCE   (— *addr u*)
Returns the address and length of the current input stream.

REFILL   (— *flag*)
Attempts to refill the current input buffer, either from the keyboard or, when **SOURCE-ID** is non-zero, from the file indicated by its *fileid*. *flag* is true if the operation succeeded.

EVALUATE (*i*x addr u — *j*x)

Makes the string at *addr u* the current input buffer and interprets it. Stack comments *i*x and *j*x represent possible parameters and results, respectively.

Try this To see the operation of **EVALUATE**, type the following:

```
: TRY ( -- )  PAD 80 BLANK  1 WORD COUNT PAD SWAP MOVE ;
: DO-IT   PAD 80 -TRAILING EVALUATE ;
TRY 1024 16 /MOD . .
DO-IT
```

EVALUATE typically is used to pass a command string to another task (or even to a remote Forth system), or to process a command string acquired from a source other than the normal input stream (such as a Windows dialog box).

8.4 Compiler

The action of the words **:** and **;** have been implied throughout this book. Each of them actually has two behaviors, one at compile time and another at run time.

```
: NAME    <words> ;
```

At compile time, the word **:** is executed. It makes a new dictionary entry (e.g., using **CREATE**) and sets a smudge bit in the name field to prevent unintended recursion (the word **RECURSE** may be used in the definition if the word must call itself). Then **:** proceeds by compiling the words making up the definition into the body of the word being defined. The exceptions to this are immediate words and literal values that execute at compile-time. The run-time behavior of **:** is responsible for causing the instructions at these addresses to be executed.

The compile time behavior of the word **;** is to un-smudge the definition (making it findable in the current search order) and to compile run-time code to exit the definition so the word can return to its caller.

8.4.1 Compiler Control

As we will soon see, it is sometimes useful to be able to turn the compiler off and on while compiling a colon definition. The words that do this are:

• **[** terminates compilation, begins text interpretation.
• **]** terminates interpretation, begins compilation.

The definitions of **:** and **;** use these words to perform the described action. The most common usage of **[** and **]** is to temporarily leave compile mode to perform some action or operation that can't be done while compiling.

One use of this strategy is for handling literals. A literal is a numeric character string that is to be compiled directly into a definition or into some other form.

When Forth finds a number while compiling a colon definition, it converts the number to its binary representation and compiles it as a literal. The most common form of a compiled literal contains code to push the contents of the value onto the stack.

The word **LITERAL** is used to construct a literal at compile-time. For example, the expression 1024 16 / has a constant value of 64. The definition:

```
: SLOW ( -- n )   1024 16 / ;
```

...will likely perform the divide every time the definition is executed and will take up extra bytes of dictionary space.[15] A better way to do this is by doing the arithmetic at compile time. The words [and] allow compile-time arithmetic and other operations within a : definition.

```
: FAST ( -- n )   [ 1024 16 / ]   LITERAL ;
```

When [is encountered, compilation stops and the interpreter pushes the two values onto the stack, performs the division, and leaves the result 64 on the stack. Then] resumes compilation, and the word **LITERAL** compiles the 64 from the stack into the dictionary. When **FAST** is executed, **LITERAL** pushes the contents of the next cell in the dictionary onto the stack. There are several advantages to this method. First, it is faster because the arithmetic is performed only once. Second, it uses less dictionary space.

This scheme can also be used to document the origin or derivation of a number. For example:

```
<words>  [ #MEALS #DAYS * ]   LITERAL   <more words> ...
```

...makes sense as a number of meals per day times the number of serving days, both previously defined as constants. The arithmetic product itself might be less meaningful if it were inserted as a numeric literal.

8.4.2 Nameless Definitions

It is occasionally useful to make a definition without a name. An example might be a default behavior for a **DEFER** or other situations in which you require access to the *xt* of a definition but have no need for a name. Of course, in most such cases, having a superfluous name is not harmful, but you may wish to avoid it to save space or to provide a measure of security.

The word **:NONAME** begins compiling a definition which is, in most respects, identical to a normal colon definition — but it has no head. Instead, its *xt* is left on the stack. For example:

```
:NONAME ( -- )   1 ABORT" Uninitialized vector" ;
VALUE DEFAULT   DEFER ACTION   DEFAULT IS ACTION
```

Here, the *xt* returned by **:NONAME** is the argument to **VALUE**, becoming the value returned by **DEFAULT**. It is used to initialize **ACTION** and may be used to reset it or to initialize other **DEFER** words.

---

15. Some Forth implementations, like SwiftForth and many of the SwiftX cross-compilers, have built-in optimizing compilers that will automatically substitute such an expression with its literal value.

8.4.3 Problem: ?WAY Revisited Yet Again

Convert your **?WAY** problem (Section 3.5.5, Section 5.4.1,Section 7.2.1) to use vectored execution, using your input key (I, J, K, L, M) as a selector. Use **:NONAME** for this revision of **?WAY**.

8.5 Exceptions and Error Handling

There are two layers of exception-handling words in Forth. The high-level words described in the Section 8.5.1 have been in Forth for many years. The more flexible, low-level words in Section 8.5.2 were added by ANS Forth in 1994.

8.5.1 High-level Abort Routines

Frequently, when an interactive Forth task aborts, it is desirable to display a message, clear the stacks, and re-enter a default state awaiting user commands. Three routines handle abort conditions for interactive Forth tasks:

Glossary

ABORT $(i^*x -) (R: j^*x -)$
Unconditionally stops execution, empties both stacks, and returns to the task's idle behavior. No message is issued.

ABORT" <text>" $(i^*x \, flag -)(R: j^*x -)$
If *flag* is true (non-zero), displays text, clears both stacks, and returns to the task's idle behavior. On many systems, it also displays the high-level word in which the abort occurred. Must be used inside a definition.

QUIT $(i^*x -)(R: j^*x -)$
Terminates execution of the current word (and all words that called it). Clears the return and data stacks. Enters interpretation state and begins an infinite loop awaiting text from the input source and interpreting it. **QUIT** is the default idle behavior for interactive Forth tasks.

8.5.2 Low-level Error Handling

Forth provides several error handling methods. **ABORT** and **ABORT"** may be used to detect errors. However, they are relatively inflexible: they unconditionally terminate program execution and return to the idle state. The words **CATCH** and **THROW**, discussed in this section, provide a method for propagating error handling to any desired level in an application program.

Glossary

CATCH $(i^*x\ xt - j^*x\ 0\ |\ i^*x\ n)$

Save information about the depth of the data and return stacks in an *exception frame* and push the frame onto the *exception stack*. Execute the execution token *xt* (as with **EXECUTE**). If the execution of *xt* completes normally (i.e., no **THROW** occurred), pop the exception frame and return zero on top of the data stack — above whatever stack items were returned by *xt* **EXECUTE** — and delete the stack-depth information. See the definition of **THROW** for completion of the exception-processing behavior.

THROW $(k^*x\ n - k^*x\ |\ i^*x\ n)$

If *n* is zero, simply discard it from the data stack. If *n* is non-zero, pop the top-most frame from the exception stack, restore the input-source specification that was in use before the corresponding **CATCH**, and adjust the depths of all stacks so they are the same as the depths saved in the exception frame (the value of *i* in **THROW**'s stack comments is the same as the value of *i* in **CATCH**). Place *n* on top of the data stack and transfer control to a point just beyond the corresponding **CATCH** that pushed the exception frame.

THROW may be thought of as a multi-level exit from a definition, with **CATCH** marking the location to which the **THROW** returns.

Suppose that, at some point, word A calls word B, whose execution may cause an error to occur. Instead of just executing word B, word A calls word B using the word **CATCH**. Someplace in B's definition (or in words that B may call), there is at least one instance of the word **THROW**, which executes if an error occurs, leaving a non-zero, numerical throw code identifier on the stack. After B has executed and program execution returns to word A just beyond the **CATCH**, the throw code is available on the stack to assist A in handling the error. If the **THROW** was not executed, the top stack item after the **CATCH** is zero.

When **CATCH** executes, it requires the execution token of the lower-level routine it is to call to be on top of the stack:

      … ['] <routine name> **CATCH** …

…is the typical syntax. At the time **CATCH** executes, there may be other items on the data stack. Before **CATCH** executes the word, it will save information about the current data and return stacks, and possibly other environmental data (called an *exception frame*), so that if an error occurs it can use this information to attempt a recovery.

After the routine called via **CATCH** has executed and control has returned to the routine that did the **CATCH**, there are two possible situations. If the lower-level routine (and any words it called) did not cause a **THROW** to execute, the top stack item after the **CATCH** will be zero and the remainder of the data stack may be different than it was before, changed by the behavior of the lower-level routine. If a **THROW** did occur, the top stack item after the **CATCH** will contain the non-zero throw code, and the remainder of the data stack will be restored to the same depth (although not necessarily to the same data) it had just before the **CATCH**. The return stack will also be restored to the depth it had before the **CATCH**.

When **THROW** executes, it takes a *throw code* from the top of the stack. If this code is zero, THROW does nothing except to remove the zero; the remainder of the stack is unchanged. If the throw code is non-zero, THROW returns the code on top of the stack, restores the data stack depth (but not necessarily the data) to its value when CATCH was executed, restores the return stack depth, and passes control back to the routine that made the CATCH. If a non-zero THROW occurs without a corresponding application-program CATCH to return to, it is treated as an ABORT.

Exception frames are placed on an exception stack in order to allow nesting of CATCH and THROW. Each use of CATCH pushes an exception frame onto the exception stack. If execution proceeds normally, CATCH pops the frame; if an error occurs, THROW pops the frame and uses its information for restoration.

An example of CATCH and THROW taken from ANS Forth is:

```
: COULD-FAIL ( -- c) KEY DUP [CHAR] Q = IF
  1 THROW THEN ;
: DO-IT ( n n -- c) 2DROP COULD-FAIL ;
: TRY-IT ( -- ) 1 2 ['] DO-IT CATCH IF
  2DROP ." There was an exception" CR
  ELSE ." The character was " EMIT CR THEN ;
```

The upper-level word TRY-IT calls the high-risk operation DO-IT (which, in turn, calls COULD-FAIL) using CATCH. Following the CATCH, the data stack contains either the character returned by KEY and a zero on top, or two otherwise-undefined items (to restore it to its depth prior to the CATCH) and a 1 on top. any non-zero value is interpreted as true, the returned throw code is suitable for direct input to the IF clause in TRY-IT.

As a further example of the use of CATCH and THROW, here is a possible implementation of our ?WAY problem:

```
: KEYCASE ( -- )
  KEY  CASE
    [CHAR] I OF <"up" code> ENDOF
    [CHAR] J OF <"left" code> ENDOF
    ( etc. )
    $1B ( esc) OF  123 THROW  ENDOF
    DUP EMIT
  ENDCASE ;
: SAFE-WAY ( -- )
  BEGIN  ['] KEYCASE CATCH
    DUP IF  DUP 123 <> IF  THROW ( error )
      ELSE ." Escaped!"
      THEN THEN
  ( 0 or 123) UNTIL ;
```

Note that the code following the CATCH in SAFE-WAY checks whether the throw code that was returned is one we're prepared to process here; if it is not, it just does a THROW to a higher CATCH. You may similarly place a CATCH around any application word that may generate an exception whose management you wish to control. Typically, a CATCH is followed by a CASE statement to process possible THROW codes that may be returned, although if you are only interested in one or two possible THROW codes at this level, an IF ... THEN structure may be more appropriate, as in our example. This strategy lets you handle errors at whatever level in an application is best positioned to take appropriate action.

It's highly advisable to have a **CATCH** around the highest-level word in your application to handle any **THROW** that wasn't handled at a lower level. At the top level of SwiftForth, the text interpreter provides a **CATCH** around the interpretation of each line processed. SwiftForth handles errors detected by the text interpreter's **CATCH** by displaying a descriptive error message in the debug window. We recommend that the highest level in your application provide a global **CATCH**, as well, for any exceptions you have not elected to handle at lower levels.

Certain negative throw codes have been given special meaning by Standard Forth, as shown in the table below. Not all of these potential exceptions are actually checked for, in most implementations, but their codes are reserved and should not be used for any other purpose. Other negative codes are available to the system for system-handled events. Positive throw codes are available for application use.

Table 7: Throw codes

Code	Meaning
-1	**ABORT**
-2	**ABORT"**
-3	stack overflow
-4	stack underflow
-5	return stack overflow
-6	return stack underflow
-7	do-loops nested too deeply during execution
-8	dictionary overflow
-9	invalid memory address
-10	division by zero
-11	result out of range
-12	argument type mismatch
-13	undefined word
-14	interpreting a compile-only word
-15	invalid **FORGET**
-16	attempt to use zero-length string as a name
-17	pictured numeric output string overflow
-18	parsed string overflow
-19	definition name too long
-20	write to a read-only location
-21	unsupported operation (e.g., **AT-XY** on a too-dumb terminal)
-22	control structure mismatch
-23	address alignment exception
-24	invalid numeric argument
-25	return stack imbalance
-26	loop parameters unavailable

Table 7: Throw codes *(continued)*

Code	Meaning
-27	invalid recursion
-28	user interrupt
-29	compiler nesting
-30	obsolescent feature
-31	>BODY used on non-CREATEd definition
-32	invalid name argument (e.g., TO xxx)
-33	block read exception
-34	block write exception
-35	invalid block number
-36	invalid file position
-37	file I/O exception
-38	non-existent file
-39	unexpected end of file
-40	invalid BASE for floating point conversion
-41	loss of precision
-42	floating-point divide by zero
-43	floating-point result out of range
-44	floating-point stack overflow
-45	floating-point stack underflow
-46	floating-point invalid argument
-47	compilation word list deleted
-48	invalid POSTPONE
-49	search-order overflow
-50	search-order underflow
-51	compilation word list changed
-52	control-flow stack overflow
-53	exception stack overflow
-54	floating-point underflow
-55	floating-point unidentified fault
-56	QUIT
-57	exception in sending or receiving a character
-58	[IF], [ELSE], or [THEN] exception

8.6 Defining Words

The most unique feature of Forth, the most powerful, and often the most difficult for students to grasp, is its ability to create new classes of words and to specify the run-time behavior of the instances of those classes.

We have seen a number of defining words so far. Each has associated with it two behaviors:

- One is exhibited when the defining word itself is executed to make a new instance of its class of words. We call that its *defining behavior*.
- The other is the behavior shared by all instances of this class when they are executed. We call that its *instance behavior*.

Glossary   This glossary summarizes some of the defining words we're already familiar with.

:   (—)

Makes a definition whose content consists of a list of procedure calls, terminated by **;**. A word defined by **:** executes the procedures in the order specified.

CREATE   (—)

Makes a definition associated with the next location in data space (but doesn't allot any space). A word defined by **CREATE** pushes onto the stack the address of the associated data space (i.e. the *parameter field address*).

VARIABLE   (—)

Makes a definition associated with the next location in data space. Allots one cell of data space. A word defined by **VARIABLE** pushes the address of it data space onto the stack.

2VARIABLE   (—)

Like **VARIABLE**, but allots two cells of data space.

VALUE   (x —)

Makes a definition with a specified single-cell value x. A word defined by **VALUE** pushes its current value onto the stack (unlike a word defined by **VARIABLE**, which pushes its address).

CONSTANT   (x —)

Makes a definition with a specified single-cell value *x*. A word defined by **CONSTANT** pushes the value onto the stack.

2CONSTANT   (x1 x2 —)

Makes a definition with a specified cell pair. A word defined by **2CONSTANT** pushes the two cells onto the stack in the same order in which they were provided when the definition was made.

The form of a defining word is:

```
: <name>    <defining behavior>
  DOES>    <instance behavior> ;
```

The defining behavior must include **CREATE** or a word that calls **CREATE**. The word **DOES>** terminates the defining behavior, and sets the instance behavior of all words defined by *name* to the words following **DOES>**. When the instance behavior begins to execute, the address of the data space associated with the instance will be pushed on the stack, on top of any explicit parameters the instance may expect.

As an example, one might define **2CONSTANT** this way:

```
: 2CONSTANT ( n1 n2 -- )   CREATE  , ,
   DOES> ( -- n1 n2 )   2@ ;
```

As a general rule, we don't show in the stack comment the instance address for the **DOES>** part of the definition. This stack comment is intended to show a user how to use these words, and it isn't the user's responsibility to provide this address.

For example, the definition:

```
: ARRAY ( n -- )   CREATE  DUP , CELLS ALLOT
   DOES>  ( n -- a)  SWAP OVER @ OVER < OVER
     1 < OR  ABORT" Out of Range"  CELLS + ;
```

...will create a new class of words whose instance behavior (following **DOES>**) is to index into an array, after verifying that the requested index *n* is valid. Its usage is:

```
10 ARRAY F-STOP
 7 ARRAY SHUTTER
 4 ARRAY ASA
```

The words **F-STOP**, **SHUTTER**, and **ASA** are instances of the class **ARRAY**. All will have the same behavior, just as each word defined with **CONSTANT** will have the same behavior (namely, to push its value on the stack). If our application is a computer-controlled camera, we will need various values of **F-STOP**, **SHUTTER** speed, and **ASA** film speed. We will store into or retrieve those values by index number:

```
3 SHUTTER
```

...will return the address of the third shutter setting. Let's discuss how this works.

The defining behavior of the word **ARRAY** is to save space for the number of values that will fit into the array, and to **ALLOT** that many **CELLS** in the dictionary. The word **DOES>** marks the end of the defining behavior. All the words following **DOES>** in the definition make up the instance behavior, i.e., these words will be executed *when an instance of this class of words is executed*. The instance's action (**SHUTTER**, for example) is to retrieve the number of entries in the table, to verify that the requested offset is within the table and, if it is, to compute the address. The relationship of the dictionary entries for **ARRAY** and the member word **SHUTTER** is shown in Figure 17.

Figure 17. Defining word's defining and instance behaviors

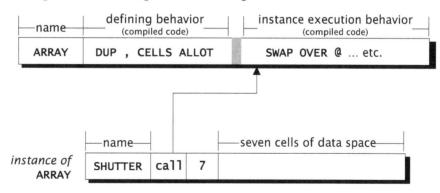

The various time sequences for this definition of **ARRAY** are shown in Figure 18.

Figure 18. Defining words, execution sequence.

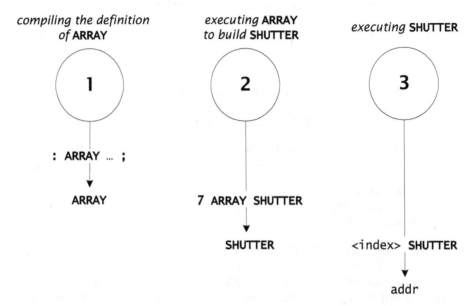

8.6.1 Problem: 2ARRAY

We have just seen an example of the use of a defining word to create one-dimensional arrays. Now create a defining word named **2ARRAY** that will be used to define a class of two-dimensional arrays in the following way:

    <n1> <n2> 2ARRAY <name>

...where *n1* is the number of rows, *n2* is the number of columns, and *name* is the name of the new array. Remember that the cell referred to by 2 3 is not the same as that referred to by 3 2!

The compile-time portion of **2ARRAY** must **CREATE** a header in the dictionary and **ALLOT** the correct number of cells. The run-time portion of **2ARRAY** expects two parameters on the stack, which must be used to compute the index into the array and return the address of the indexed cell.

8.6.2 Summary of Defining Words

    CREATE
    DOES>
    VARIABLE
    2VARIABLE
    CONSTANT
    2CONSTANT

Section 9: File Operations

9.1 The File-Access Word Set

Most modern Forth implementations run under host operating systems (such as SwiftForth, which runs under Windows, Linux, and macOS). ANS Forth introduced a useful set of general-purpose words for accessing host OS files, whether they are used for program source or data storage, called the File Wordset. The most important of these are discussed in this section; a more extensive treatment of the File Wordset may be found in *Forth Programmer's Handbook*.

The File Wordset depends on several basic assumptions and special terms:

- Files are provided by a host operating system.
- File state information (e.g., current position in the file, size, etc.) is managed by the OS. File sizes are dynamically variable, so write operations will increase the size of a file as necessary.
- Filenames are represented as character strings. The format of the names is determined by the host operating system. Filenames may include system-specific pathnames.
- A *file identifier (fileid)* is a single-cell value passed to file operators to refer to specific files. The nature of a *fileid* value depends on the host OS. Opening a file assigns it a file identifier, which remains valid until the file is closed. When the text interpreter is using a file as the input, its *fileid* will be returned by **SOURCE-ID**. The other possible values that **SOURCE-ID** can return are zero (if the user input device is the source), and -1 (if the source is a character string passed by **EVALUATE**). See Section 8.3 for information about the text interpreter.
- File contents are accessed as a sequence of characters. The *file position* is the character offset from the start of the file. The file position is updated by all read, write, and reposition commands.
- File read operations return an *actual* transfer count, which can differ from the *requested* transfer count.
- A *file access method (fam)* is a single-cell value indicating a permissible means of accessing a specific file, such as read/write or read-only.
- An *I/O result (ior)* is a single-cell value indicating the result of an I/O operation. A value of zero indicates success; the meanings of non-zero values are defined by the host OS. An operation reaching the end of a file is not considered an error and returns a zero *ior*.

9.1.1 File Status and Parameters

These are the words used to query file status. Note that the parameters for file position and size are *unsigned double-cell* integers; this allows for reasonably large file sizes even on 16-bit implementations.

FILE-POSITION (*fileid — ud ior*)

Returns the current file position *ud* and an *ior*. If *ior* is non-zero (indicating an error), *ud* is undefined.

FILE-SIZE (*fileid — ud ior*)

Returns the file size *ud* and an *ior*. This operation does not affect the value returned by **FILE-POSITION**. If the *ior* is non-zero, *ud* is undefined.

FILE-STATUS (*addr u — x ior*)

Returns the status of the file whose name is given by the character string at *addr* and whose length is *u*. The returned *ior* = 0 if the file exists, otherwise it's a system-dependent value. The returned value *x* contains system-dependent file status.

9.1.2 Managing Files

The words described in this section perform the basic operations for creating and managing files. When creating and opening files, you can specify a "file access method" or *fam*. These are specified by pre-defined constants (whose actual values are system-dependent), as follows:

- **R/W** Read/write
- **R/O** Read only
- **W/O** Write only

Any of these may be followed by **BIN**, which additionally specifies that the file is a binary file.[16]

CLOSE-FILE (*fileid — ior*)

Closes the file identified by *fileid*.

CREATE-FILE (*addr u fam — fileid ior*)

Creates a file, whose name is the string *addr u*, and opens it with file access method *fam*. If the file already exists, it will be re-created as an empty file. If the operation succeeds, *ior* = 0, otherwise *ior* is non-zero and *fileid* is undefined.

DELETE-FILE (*addr u — ior*)

Deletes the file whose name is given by the character string *addr u*.

FLUSH-FILE (*fileid — ior*)

Forces any buffered contents of the file referenced by *fileid* to be written to mass storage, and updates the size information for the file, if changed.

OPEN-FILE (*addr u fam — fileid ior*)

Opens the file whose name is given by the character string *addr u*, with file access

---

16. In the Windows, Linux, and macOS operating systems, there is no distinction made between binary and text files, so **BIN** in SwiftForth is a no-op.

method *fam*. If opening is successful, sets the file position to zero, and returns an *ior* of zero and the *fileid*; otherwise, returns a non-zero *ior* and an undefined value for *fileid*.

RENAME-FILE   (*addr1 u1 addr2 u2 — ior*)

Renames the file whose current name is given by the string *addr1 u1*, to the name given by the character string at *addr2 u2*.

RESIZE-FILE   (*ud fileid — ior*)

Sets the size of the file identified by *fileid* to *ud*, and return an *ior*. If the file size is increased, the content of the newly allocated space is indeterminate. After successful completion, **FILE-SIZE** returns the same value for *ud*, and **FILE-POSITION** returns an undefined value.

Note   Passing the name of a file that already exists to **CREATE-FILE** causes that file to be opened and its length truncated to 0 (as if it were just created). If this is not what you intended, do an **OPEN-FILE** or **FILE-STATUS** first, and if that fails (i.e., the file does not already exist), then do a **CREATE-FILE**.

The words that use text strings for file names typically get them either from the command line (using **WORD** or **PARSE**) or by using **S"** (either inside a colon definition or interpretively).

Try this   Pick one of your classwork files to use for this exercise:

```
S" <filename>" R/O OPEN-FILE .
```

This will open your file and display the resulting *ior*, which should be zero. The value that remains on the stack is the *fileid*, generally the file handle returned by the OS. Type **.S** to display the *fileid* without removing it from the stack.

Now, using this *fileid* as your argument, type:

```
FILE-SIZE . D.
```

This should display another zero *ior*, followed by your file size. Is that correct?

If you will be working with the file for a while (which is normally the case in an application), you'll want to save your *fileid* in a **VARIABLE** or **VALUE**.

With the *fileid* on the stack, close your file:

```
<fileid> CLOSE-FILE .
```

...yielding a final zero *ior*.

9.1.3 Reading and Writing Files

The following words provide basic access to data in files. Note that **READ-LINE** and **WRITE-LINE** are only appropriate for text (not binary) files.

READ-FILE   (*addr u1 fileid — u2 ior*)

Reads up to *u1* characters from the file referenced by *fileid* to the buffer at *addr*, and updates **FILE-POSITION**. The return value *u2* is the number of characters successfully read. If no exception occurred, *ior* = 0 and *u2* = *u1* or the number of characters actually read before encountering the end of the file, whichever is smaller. If **FILE-POSITION** was equal to **FILE-SIZE** before executing **READ-FILE**, *u2* is zero. If *ior* is non-zero, *u2* is the number of characters successfully transferred before the exception occurred.

READ-LINE   (*addr u1 fileid — u2 flag ior*)

Reads a line up to *u1* consecutive characters from the file referenced by *fileid* into a buffer at *addr*, and updates **FILE-POSITION**. Terminates if a line-end is encountered. The return value *u2* is the actual number of characters read, not including the line-end (if any). One or two line-ends may be read into memory at the end of the line in addition to *u2*, so the buffer at *addr* should be at least *u1*+2 characters long. If *n2* = *u1*, the line-end was not reached. If no exception occurred, *ior* = 0 and *flag* is true. If **FILE-POSITION** was equal to **FILE-SIZE** before executing **READ-LINE**, *flag* is false, *ior* = 0, and *u2* = 0. If *ior* is non-zero, the remaining returned parameters are undefined.

WRITE-FILE   (*addr u fileid — ior*)

Writes *u* characters from *addr* to the file referenced by *fileid*, starting at its current file position, increasing **FILE-SIZE** if necessary. After this operation, **FILE-POSITION** will return the position just after the last character written, and **FILE-SIZE** will return a value equal to or greater than **FILE-POSITION**.

WRITE-LINE   (*addr u fileid — ior*)

Writes *u* characters from *addr* to the file referenced by *fileid*, starting at its current file position, increasing **FILE-SIZE** if necessary. The text is followed by a line-end. After this operation, **FILE-POSITION** will return the next file position after the last character written to the file, and **FILE-SIZE** will return a value equal to or greater than **FILE-POSITION**.

Try this   Here's some code that will read and display a line from the current position in a file:

```
258 BUFFER: LINE-BUF

: ECHO-LINE ( fileid -- flag )   \ Display 1 line
   LINE-BUF 256 ROT READ-LINE DROP\ n chars, flag
   CR  LINE-BUF ROT TYPE ;
```

You could use this in a word to display all lines in a file, like this:

```
: SHOW-FILE ( addr u -- )
   R/O OPEN-FILE ABORT" Can't open file"
   BEGIN  DUP ( fileid) ECHO-LINE  0= UNTIL
   ( fileid) CLOSE-FILE DROP ;
```

...and add a user-interface word:

```
: SHOW ( -- )                        \ Usage:  SHOW <filename>
   1 WORD COUNT SHOW-FILE ;
```

9.1.4 Interpreting Files

Most applications don't need to interpret files, but it can be convenient to use a text file to provide a script or other material to the Forth interpreter. To do so, you temporarily redirect the input stream to the file. The following words are meant for this.

Glossary

INCLUDE-FILE   (*fileid* —)
Reads and interprets the file referenced by *fileid*, line by line, until the end of file is reached. When the end of the file is reached, closes the file and restores the previous input stream specification.

INCLUDED   (*addr u* —)
Same as **INCLUDE-FILE**, except it first opens the file specified by its name, which is given by the text string *addr u*.

INCLUDE <filename>   (—)
Like **INCLUDE-FILE**, but the file is specified by the filename that follows in the input.

Overall management of the input stream will be discussed further in Section 8.3.

9.1.5 Text File Problems

1. Select one of your existing classwork files. Define **SHOW** to display each line in the file on which a specified string occurs. For example, if you type:

   SHOW DUP

   ...you should see each line on which **DUP** occurs.

2. Make a word **IN** that can be followed by a filename, for example:

   IN MYFILE.F

   It should select this file as the target for **SHOW** above. Modify **SHOW** to use this file.

3. Make a new file, and write a word **COPY** that works like **SHOW** except that instead of displaying the selected lines it copies them to the new file.

Tip   Don't forget to close your files when you're finished with them.

Section 10: Multitasking

This entire section is specific to FORTH, Inc. products, describing the multitasking model used in polyFORTH, chipFORTH, and SwiftX as well as the model adapted for the Windows environment in SwiftForth.

10.1 Basic Principles

The multitasker in Forth, as in other operating system environments, is responsible for apportioning system resources among *tasks*, concurrent processes running on the host CPU. Any multitasker must provide certain support functions; that is, the system itself has two personalities:

- The virtual machine wherein each task appears to command the full system.
- The actual machine wherein all tasks act as an interrelated and complex program sharing resources and information.

Depending on one's point of view, the job of using a multitasking operating system can be difficult and cumbersome or simple and straightforward. The implementation of an operating system can, likewise, make it hard or easy for a programmer to implement a given task.

In order for tasks to appear to run concurrently and transparently, the OS must distribute resources fairly among all users of the CPU. These resources include:

- CPU time: how long each task may run uninterrupted.
- I/O: how a task communicates with the outside world.
- Storage: memory allocation in RAM for code and data.
- Interrupts: handling of external, asynchronous requests for the system.

There are three common models for managing multitasking:

- Time-slicing: the CPU is allocated to tasks for a specified period of time.
- Event-driven: a task can use the CPU until an event occurs (e.g., a hardware or software interrupt) that causes a higher-priority task to request it.
- Cooperative: a task runs until it relinquishes the CPU voluntarily.

Within each of these, there may also be various mechanisms for determining which task gets the CPU next if the running task relinquishes it.

The first two models above are *pre-emptive* — the OS can take the CPU away from a running task without the task's knowledge or consent. This means the OS must preserve extensive context information (e.g., all registers, temporary buffers, etc.), which significantly slows down the context switch. It also complicates inter-task communication. For example, if two tasks want to share a **2VARIABLE** in common memory, it's conceivable that one task can be halfway through a **2!** when the other task performs a **2@**, getting a wrong result.

A cooperative model has the advantage of very fast context switches, as far less information has to be saved and restored; however it has the disadvantage that a task could monopolize the CPU. The ideal model would be a cooperative model that has a way of ensuring adequate service to all tasks.

FORTH, Inc. has two approaches to multitasking:

- In embedded systems, we offer SwiftOS (or pF/x on our older polyFORTH and chip-FORTH systems). This is a cooperative, *round-robin* multitasker that features maximum performance and programmer control of task swapping.
- Under a multitasking OS (Windows, Linux, macOS), we have provided a high-level interface to multiple execution threads. It has an API similar to SwiftOS, but works within the host OS programming paradigm. These are quite different, so we'll discuss each separately.

10.2 The SwiftOS Multitasker

The SwiftOS multitasker is used in FORTH, Inc.'s SwiftX cross-development environment for embedded systems. This is the same multitasker named pF/x in poly-FORTH and chipFORTH products from 1978 through 1995. It has been proven in hundred of thousands of instances, in many thousands of applications, on a wide variety of microprocessors and microcontrollers.

10.2.1 SwiftOS Principles

SwiftOS solves several problems with its simple, fast multitasking scheme. SwiftOS is a cooperative multitasker, so it achieves the benefits of fast context switches and full programmer control. It minimizes the likelihood that any task can monopolize the CPU by establishing the simple rule that all I/O operations include at least one **PAUSE**, which allows other tasks to run. Because I/O is a frequent occurrence in embedded and real-time applications, and because I/O operations are relatively time consuming when measured in CPU cycles, most tasks spend most of their time suspended — waiting for I/O — so no task wishing to run has to wait long. For infrequent situations that require CPU-intensive activity (e.g., long sorts or complex mathematical calculations), it's easy to **PAUSE** in CPU-intensive functions to ensure that other tasks have the opportunity to run.

Tasks are arranged in a *round robin*, which means each task on the system is given a chance to use all the resources of the system before relinquishing control to the next task in line (Figure 19). In SwiftOS, the programmer always knows exactly when a task does and does not relinquish the CPU. Context switches always occur between Forth words, so the job of saving and restoring is quite fast: on most processors, a complete context switch can be done in just a few machine instructions.

Figure 19. Tasks in a round-robin multitasker

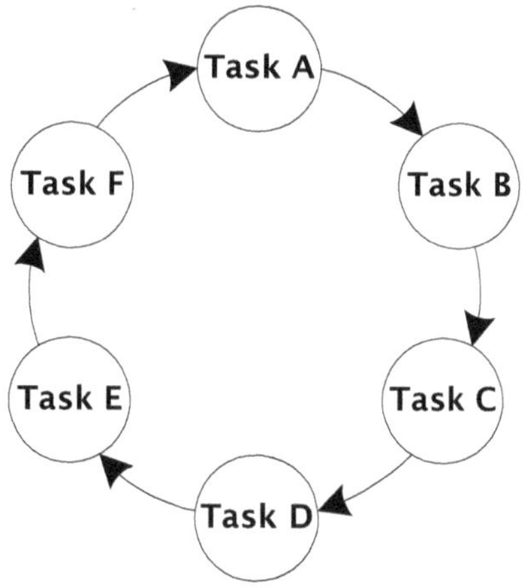

This scheduling and allocation scheme results in the following characteristics:

- CPU time: each task gets as much time as it needs. During input or output, the system is available to other tasks.
- I/O: terminal I/O is normally interrupt-driven, or may be a combination of interrupt-driven queued serial input and polled output.
- Storage: tasks have fixed memory partitions.
- Interrupts: serviced with minimum overhead; effects are easier to track because of the minimal machine state to be aware of.

10.2.2 Task Definition and Control

There are two phases to task management: definition and instantiation. When a task is defined, it gets a dictionary entry containing a Task Control Block (TCB), which is the table containing its size and other parameters. This happens when a program is compiled, and the task's definition and TCB are permanent parts of the dictionary. In a cross-compiler such as SwiftX, the TCB has an entry in the host's dictionary, and values in the target's initialized data space.

In SwiftX, tasks are typically instantiated and assigned their behaviors as part of the power-up initialization sequence in the target. Instantiation and assignment of function are separate actions. When a task is instantiated, it is given a region of RAM called its user area, which is initialized by values from the TCB but which also contains dynamic information reflecting the activity of the task. Individual entries in the task's user area are called *user variables*. The task also gets its own data and return stacks.

After SwiftOS has instantiated a task, it may communicate with it via the shared memory that is visible to both SwiftOS and the task, or via the task's user variables.

User variables are defined by USER, which takes an offset relative to the start of the task's user area. About a dozen user variables are required by the system for a background task; more are required for a terminal task. Additional user variables may be defined for application use. User variables differ from normal variables only in that each task has its own private copy of its data space.

SwiftOS supports two kinds of tasks:

1. Control or background tasks
2. Terminal tasks

The difference is that terminal tasks have a much larger user area, enabling them to perform serial I/O using **TYPE**, etc. Control tasks are primarily for tasks performing simple functions such as monitoring custom I/O in targets where memory conservation is important.

Control tasks are defined with the word **BACKGROUND** and are instantiated by **BUILD**, whereas terminal tasks are defined by **TERMINAL** and are instantiated by **CONSTRUCT**. These words are discussed in the glossary below.

The action of assigning an activity to a task must be done inside a colon definition, using the form:

```
: <name> <taskname> ACTIVATE <words to execute> ;
```

When *name* is executed, the task *taskname* will begin executing the words that follow **ACTIVATE**.

The task's assigned behavior, represented above by "words to execute," may be one of two types:

1. transitory behavior, which the task simply executes and then terminates; and
2. persistent behavior, represented by an infinite loop the task will perform forever (e.g., **BEGIN** … **AGAIN**).

Transitory behavior must be terminated by the word **STOP**, which leaves the task disabled until it gets a new job assignment with another **ACTIVATE**.

Persistent behavior must include the infinite loop and, within that loop, provision must be made for the task to relinquish the CPU using **PAUSE**, **STOP**, or a word that calls one of these (such as **MS** or any I/O word such as **TYPE**, **EMIT**, **KEY**, etc.). These words are also discussed in the glossary below.

Whether the task's behavior is persistent or transient, the programmer must always ensure that a task will never reach the semicolon that terminates the definition in which its behavior is assigned with **ACTIVATE**.

Glossary   The following glossary summarizes the words used in SwiftOS to define and control tasks.

BACKGROUND <name>   (*nu ns nr* —)
Defines the background task *name* — with *nu* bytes of user area, *ns* bytes of data stack, and *nr* bytes of return stack — and sets up its task control block based on these parameters. Use of *name* returns the address of its TCB.

BUILD   (*addr* —)
Initializes the task at *addr* that was constructed by **BACKGROUND**. The task will be linked in the round-robin following **OPERATOR**, and will be linked to the task previously linked to **OPERATOR**. This must be done at run time in the target system before any attempt to **ACTIVATE** the task.

Usage: <taskname> **BUILD**

TERMINAL <name>   (*n* —)
Defines the terminal task *name* and sets up its task control block; the task will have *n* bytes of working storage. Use of *name* returns the address of the task definition table, which contains the parameters for building the task.

CONSTRUCT   (*addr* —)
Initializes a task that was constructed by **TERMINAL**. The task will be linked in the round-robin following **OPERATOR**, and will be linked to the task previously linked to **OPERATOR**. This must be done at run time in the target system, before any attempt to **ACTIVATE** the task.

Usage: <taskname> **CONSTRUCT**

OPERATOR   (*addr* —)
Returns the address of the task definition table of the first task defined in the kernel. **OPERATOR** is a **TERMINAL** task.

ACTIVATE   (*addr* —)
Starts the task at *addr* executing the words following **ACTIVATE**. **ACTIVATE** may only be used inside a colon definition. The task executing the balance of the definition must be prevented from ever returning from the definition. The task may execute an infinite loop that describes its desired behavior, or use **STOP** or **NOD**.

NOD   (—)
Infinite loop designed to ensure a task remains inactive until assigned a new behavior with **ACTIVATE**.

HALT   (*addr* —)
Cause the task at *addr* to perform **NOD**.

Usage: <taskname> **HALT**

If you are programming in SwiftX or chipFORTH, keep in mind which aspects of task creation and control take place at target-compilation time (producing definitions and tables in ROM) and which are executed in the ROM target system to initialize and affect RAM.

SwiftOS is discussed in more detail in the *SwiftX Reference Manual*, and the documentation for each target includes examples of custom device drivers that meet the SwiftOS requirement that each I/O operation has to relinquish the CPU.

10.2.3 Application Examples

The following example show how SwiftOS tasks are constructed and activated.

```
{ ========================================================================
SwiftOS MULTITASKING example

In this example we define two minimum background tasks, which will
be asked to increment the user variable EVENTS, by the phrase:
    <taskname> GO.

 Because EVENTS is a USER variable, each task has its own copy.
 When the count goes negative (at 32768 on a 16-bit target, which this
 is assumed to be) the tasks will stop.

 Adjusting #DELAY will make both tasks run faster or slower. Use of MS
 causes the task to PAUSE so others can run.

 Monitor either task by typing:
    <taskname> <n> SEE
======================================================================== }

32 128 64 BACKGROUND TASK1    32 128 64 BACKGROUND TASK2
\ Include in power-up code:   TASK1 BUILD   TASK2 BUILD

30 USER EVENTS\ To be incremented by each task
100 VALUE #DELAY\ Number of ms to delay

: DELAY ( -- )   #DELAY MS ;\ Wait #DELAY milliseconds

: ACTION ( -- )   BEGIN  1 EVENTS +!  DELAY  EVENTS @ 0< UNTIL ;

: GO ( a -- )   ACTIVATE  ACTION  NOD ;

\ To monitor a task for n delay periods, type:  <taskname> <n> SEE
: SEE ( a n -- )   0 DO CR  DUP EVENTS HIS ?  DELAY  LOOP  DROP ;
```

10.3 Multitasking Under Windows

Windows is an inherently multitasked environment. The actual task-management rules vary among the different versions of Windows, but from the perspective of SwiftForth and its applications, the interface is the same.

The most important fundamental concept is that Windows is an event-driven environment. An event may be I/O (e.g., a keystroke or mouse click), receipt of a message from another window or program, or an event generated by the OS.

A SwiftForth program can support multiple threads *and* multiple windows. A *thread* is in some respects similar to a background task in SwiftOS: it is given its own stacks and user variables, and is executing code from within the SwiftForth process's dictionary. However, because the Windows OS controls execution and task switching, there is no equivalent of the round-robin loop that is found in SwiftOS.

A *task* is a Windows thread with additional facilities assigned by SwiftForth. It may be thought of as an entity capable of independently executing Forth definitions. A task has a separate stack frame assigned to it by Windows, containing its data stack, return stack, and user variables. SwiftForth may read and write a task's user variables, but cannot modify its stacks.

10.3.1 Task Definition and Control

As in SwiftOS, there are two phases to task management: definition and instantiation. When a task is defined, it gets a dictionary entry containing a Task Control Block, or TCB, which is the table containing its size and other parameters. This happens when a program is compiled, and the task's definition and TCB are permanent parts of the dictionary.

When a SwiftForth task is instantiated, Windows is requested to allocate a private stack frame to it, within which SwiftForth sets up its data and return stacks and user variables, all of which behave essentially like those in SwiftOS. At this time, the task is also assigned its behavior, or words to execute.

After SwiftForth instantiates a task, it may communicate with it via the shared memory visible to both SwiftForth and the task, or via the task's user variables.

In SwiftForth, a task is defined using the sequence:

```
<size> TASK <taskname>
```

...where *size* is the requested size of its user area and data stack, combined. The minimum value for size is 4,096 bytes; a typical value is 8,192 bytes. The task's return stack, also used for Windows calls, is always 16,384 bytes. When invoked, *taskname* will return the address of the task's TCB.

The word **ACTIVATE**, which is used in SwiftX to assign a behavior to a task, also instantiates it in SwiftForth; there is no equivalent to the words **BUILD** and **CONSTRUCT**. Its usage is the same:

```
: <name> <taskname> ACTIVATE <words to execute> ;
```

When *name* is executed, the task *taskname* will be instantiated and will begin executing the words that follow **ACTIVATE**.

Transitory behavior in SwiftForth must be terminated by the word **TERMINATE**, which uninstantiates the task. A task that has terminated in this fashion may be instantiated again, to perform the same or a different transitory behavior. Although its stacks and user area have been discarded, the TCB remains in the dictionary.

Persistent behavior (which leaves the task instantiated for an extended period) must include an infinite loop and, within that loop, provision must be made for the task to relinquish the CPU using **PAUSE**, **STOP**, **Sleep**, or a word that calls one of these (such as **MS**). These words are discussed in the glossary below. If this is not done, the task will consume all available CPU time (subject to Windows time-slicing) and performance of all other tasks and programs will degrade.

As in SwiftOS, whether the task's behavior is transitory or persistent, the programmer must ensure that it will never reach the semicolon (or an **EXIT**) that would return from the definition that contains the **ACTIVATE**.

A task that assigns behavior to another task using **ACTIVATE** is that task's *owner*. A task may **SUSPEND** another task, **RESUME** it (after a **SUSPEND**), or **KILL** (uninstantiate) it.

A task may also **HALT** another task, causing it to cease operation permanently the next time it executes **STOP** or **PAUSE**, but leaves it instantiated. The operational distinction between **HALT** and **KILL** is that after **HALT** the task remains instantiated and will retain any settings in its user variables for its next **ACTIVATE**.

A SwiftForth task might manage one or more windows. If it does, it must frequently check its message queue and process any pending messages.

In the SwiftOS non-preemptive multitasker, the programmer has complete control over when a task may relinquish the CPU, but this is not possible in OS environments like Windows, Linux, and macOS. Occasionally, it is necessary to perform a sequence of operations that cannot be interrupted by other SwiftForth tasks. Such a sequence is called a *critical section*, and Windows can ensure that a critical section is performed without interruption. SwiftForth's API to this is in the form of a pair of words, **[C** and **C]**, which begin and end a critical section. No other SwiftForth task will be permitted to run during the execution of any functions between these two words.

Glossary   Following are the principle SwiftForth task definition and control words.

TASK <name>   (*u* —)
Defines a task whose combined user area and data stack will be *u* bytes (4,096 minimum) in size. Invoking *name* returns the address of the Task Control Block (TCB).

ACTIVATE   (*addr* —)
Instantiates the task whose TCB is at *addr*, and starts it executing the words following **ACTIVATE**. Must be used inside a definition. The words following **ACTIVATE** must be structured as an infinite loop or must end with **TERMINATE** so the semicolon at the end of the definition is never executed. Also, the code must call **PAUSE** or **STOP** so task control can function properly.

If the task was already instantiated, **ACTIVATE** will simply set it to start executing the words following **ACTIVATE** immediately after the owner next executes **PAUSE** or **STOP**.

TERMINATE   (—)
Causes the task executing this word to cease operation and release all its memory back to Windows. A task that terminates itself may be re-activated.

SUSPEND   (*addr* —)
Forces the task whose TCB is at *addr* to suspend operation indefinitely.

RESUME $(addr —)$

Causes the task whose TCB is at *addr* to resume operation at the point at which it was suspended.

HALT $(addr —)$

Causes the task whose TCB is at *addr* to cease operation permanently at the next **STOP** or **PAUSE** but to remain instantiated.

Sleep $(u — ior)$

Relinquishes the CPU for approximately *u* milliseconds. If *u* is zero, the task relinquishes the rest of its time slice (typically about 10 milliseconds). **Sleep** is a Windows call used by **MS** and **PAUSE**, and is appropriate when the task wishes to avoid checking its message queue.

KILL $(addr —)$

Causes the task whose TCB is at *addr* to cease operation and release all its memory back to Windows. A task that has been killed may be re-activated.

PAUSE $(—)$

Relinquishes the CPU while checking for messages (if the task has a message queue).

STOP $(—)$

Checks for messages (if the task has a message queue) and suspends operation indefinitely (until restarted by another task).

[C $(—)$

Begins a critical section in which other SwiftForth tasks cannot execute.

C] $(—)$

Concludes a critical section.

10.3.2 SwiftForth Multitasking Examples

The following example shows how SwiftForth tasks are constructed and activated.

The obvious difference between this code and the SwiftX example in Section 10.2.3 is that tasks are defined differently and don't need to be instantiated separately.

Also, note that the user variable EVENTS was automatically added to the end of currently defined user variables, as indicated by #USER; its size in bytes was specified and #USER was updated.

Finally, because SwiftForth is a 32-bit implementation, we added an upper limit; we couldn't count on the number circle to go negative soon enough for this example!

```
{ ================================================================
SwiftForth MULTITASKING example

In this example we define two tasks, which will be asked to increment
the user variable EVENTS, by the phrase:
      <taskname> GO.
Because EVENTS is a USER variable, each task has its own copy.

When the count exceeds LIMIT the tasks will stop.
To change the limit, type:    <new-value> TO LIMIT

Adjusting #DELAY will make both tasks run faster or slower. Use of MS
causes task to PAUSE so others can run.

Monitor either task n times by typing:
      <taskname> <n> SEE
================================================================ }

4096 TASK TASK1    4096 TASK TASK2

#USER 4 +USER EVENTS \ To be incremented by each task
TO #USER

100 VALUE #DELAY\ Number of ms to delay
10000 VALUE LIMIT\ Limit after which tasks quit

: DELAY ( -- )    #DELAY MS ;\ Wait #DELAY milliseconds

: ACTION ( -- )    0 EVENTS !  BEGIN
       1 EVENTS +!  DELAY
    EVENTS @ LIMIT = UNTIL ;

: GO ( a -- )    ACTIVATE  ACTION  NOD ;

\ To monitor a task for n delay periods, type: <taskname> <n> SEE
: SEE ( a n -- )    0 DO CR  DUP EVENTS HIS ?  DELAY LOOP    DROP ;
```

10.4 Resource Sharing

In most operating systems there is a method of locking out other tasks from the use of a specific system resource. Among commonly protected resources are:

- disk
- printers
- graphics screens
- specific data
- non-reentrant functions (such as sorts)
- application-specific device usage

This can become complex on systems that require queuing or arbitration, but a non-preemptive implementation greatly simplifies it. In SwiftForth, judicious use of critical sections along with the words described here can provide equivalent security.

The way a task knows whether a resource is available is by testing a *facility variable*. This is a normal **VARIABLE** distinguished only by its purpose. This variable represents the status of the resource:

- zero if resource is available,
- non-zero if the resource is not available.

Forth provides **GET** and **RELEASE** to handle this test.

10.4.1 Acquiring a Facility

Assume, for example, that **PRINTER** is defined as a facility variable, like this:

```
VARIABLE PRINTER
```

If one says **PRINTER GET** then:

- If **PRINTER** is zero, it is set to point to the task requesting the facility.
- If **PRINTER** is non-zero, the task keeps testing the variable until it is zero, doing a **PAUSE** after each test.

No other task can **GET** this variable until the task that owns it does a **RELEASE**.

10.4.2 Releasing a Facility

A task releases a facility by using the phrase **PRINTER RELEASE** to initiate the following steps:

- It checks to see if the resource is owned by the executing task.
- If so, it stores zero into the facility variable (making it available).
- If not, it does nothing.

Example

```
: PRINT ( -- )   PRINTER GET      \ gets resource
       'REPORT @EXECUTE            \ generates a report
       PRINTER RELEASE ;           \ frees variable
```

Glossary

GET   (*addr* —)

Obtains control of the facility variable at *addr*, after first executing **PAUSE** to allow other tasks to run. If the facility is owned by another task, the task executing **GET** will wait until the facility is available.

RELEASE   (*addr* —)

Relinquishes the facility variable at *addr*. If the task executing **RELEASE** did not previously own the facility, this operation is a no-op.

Neither SwiftX nor SwiftForth have any explicit safeguards against deadlocks, in which two (or more) tasks conflict because each wants a resource the other has.

For example:

```
: 1HANG   MUX GET   TAPE GET ;
: 2HANG   TAPE GET   MUX GET ;
```

If **1HANG** and **2HANG** are run by different tasks, the tasks could eventually deadlock.

The best way to avoid deadlocks is to get facilities one at a time, if possible. If you have to get two resources at the same time, it is safest to always request them in the same order. In the example above involving a multiplexer and tape, the programmer could save values from the multiplexer in a buffer, then move them to tape. In almost all cases, there is a simple way to avoid concurrent **GET** operations. However, in a poorly written application, the conflicting requests might occur on different nesting levels, hiding the problem until a conflict occurs.

It is better to design an application to **GET** only one resource at a time — deadlocks are impossible in that case.

The code below illustrates the concepts discussed so far by adding a facility variable named **EVENTER**. If the **OPERATOR** task (you, typing in the command window) does an **EVENTER GET**, all counting will stop until you do **EVENTER RELEASE**.

```
{ =======================================================================
SwiftForth MULTITASKING example

In this example we define two tasks, which will be asked to increment
the user variable EVENTS, by the phrase:
    <taskname> GO.

Because EVENTS is a USER variable, each task has its own copy.

 The facility VARIABLE EVENTER prevents a task from interfering with
 another's counting, and allows OPERATOR to suspend counting.

 When the count exceeds LIMIT the tasks will stop.
 To change the limit, type:   <new-value> TO LIMIT

 Adjusting #DELAY will make both tasks run faster or slower. Use of MS
 causes task to PAUSE so others can run.

 Monitor either task n times by typing:
    <taskname> <n> SEE
========================================================================= }
4096 TASK TASK1    4096 TASK TASK2

#USER 4 +USER EVENTS   TO #USER\ To be incremented by each task
100 VALUE #DELAY\ Number of ms to delay
10000 VALUE LIMIT\ Limit after which tasks quit
VARIABLE EVENTER\ Facility variable

: DELAY ( -- )   #DELAY MS ;\ Wait #DELAY milliseconds

: ACTION ( -- )   0 EVENTS !  BEGIN
    EVENTER GET  1 EVENTS +!  EVENTER RELEASE  DELAY
  EVENTS @ LIMIT = UNTIL ;

: GO ( a -- )   ACTIVATE  ACTION  NOD ;

\ To monitor a task for n delay periods, type:  <taskname> <n> SEE
: SEE ( a n -- )   0 DO CR  DUP EVENTS HIS ?  DELAY  LOOP   DROP ;
```

10.5 Application Design Issues

What should a task do? How do you assign responsibilities?

The best rule is that synchronous functions should be performed by a single task, and asynchronous ones should be processed by multiple tasks. Where there are variables in shared memory, be clear as to who can change them. The interlock problem that worries some people is irrelevant in SwiftOS, because storing into a variable isn't I/O, so there is no way you can lose the CPU in mid-operation. In Swift-Forth, you may use the critical-section strategy discussed in Section 10.3.1 to protect against possibly conflicting uses of shared memory.

Here are some specific guidelines:

- Define tasks based on their job description, much as one would with people. Look at a task as a specialist dedicated to performing a sequence of operations with minimal dependency on others.

- If a job assignment or relationship becomes too complex, look for an easier approach. In particular, if you find your application is developing complicated synchronization requirements, re-assigning responsibilities often simplifies things.

- Tasks typically reflect application responsibility rather than device-specific responsibility. Sometimes they're the same, as when a task is dedicated to acquiring data from a particular source device. But it's usually a poor idea to dedicate a task to providing disk services, for example, because it's likely to become a bottleneck. Instead, the disk should be treated as a facility shared by various tasks.

The steps to take in defining tasks are:

1. Itemize, in time sequence, the events each task must perform.
2. Write words for processing these events.
3. Define the top-layer loop the task will execute.

10.5.1 Case Study

This is an actual project submitted to FORTH, Inc. by a customer. We were given the task of developing a microprocessor-based telephone switch:

- 128 lines, 8 trunks
- Each line supports:
  - off-hook sensing
  - dial-tone generation
  - busy signal
  - touch-tone sensing
  - test for busy
  - other features

The conventional, or lateral, design approach can be illustrated by Figure 20.

Figure 20. Telephone switcher, lateral design

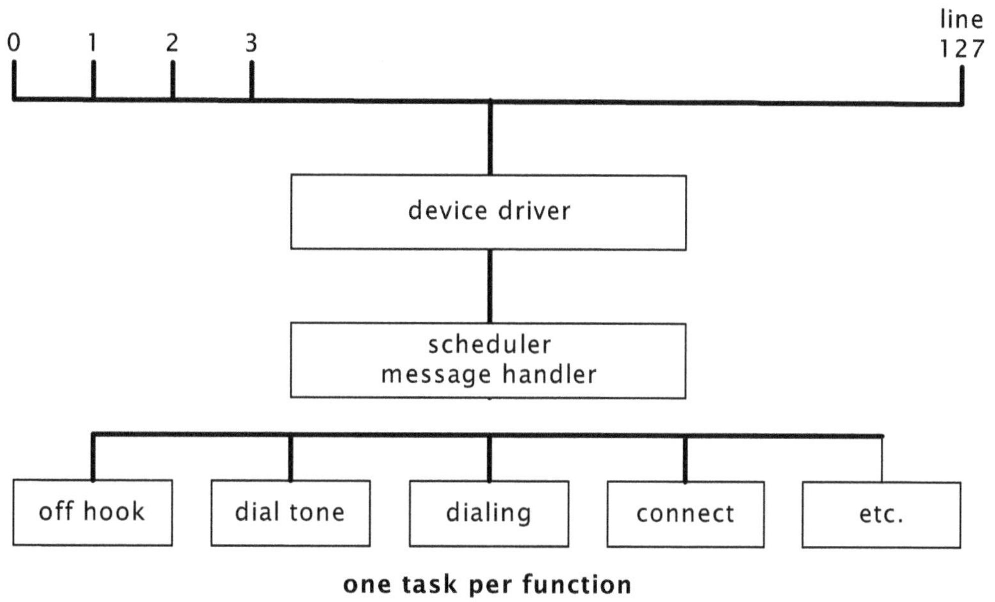

one task per function

This design was specified by the customer. It assigned one task to each function (off hook, etc.). Tasks communicated by sending messages through the scheduler/message handler.

The off-hook task was continually scanning the 128 lines to detect an off-hook condition. When one was detected, the task sent a message to the dial-tone task, which issued a dial tone and sent a message to the dialing task, etc. The customer had attempted to program this system, but the slow, 8-bit microcontroller was not keeping up with the message traffic.

We re-designed the system using the FORTH, Inc. vertical approach, as in Figure 21.

Figure 21. Telephone switcher, vertical approach

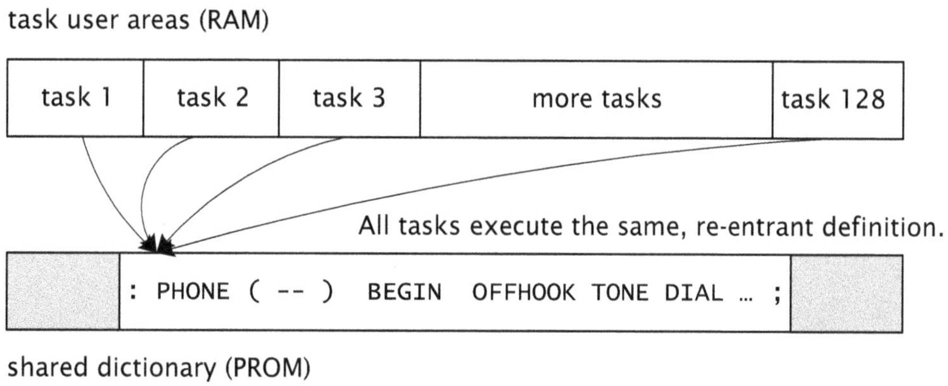

task user areas (RAM)

All tasks execute the same, re-entrant definition.

```
: PHONE ( -- )  BEGIN  OFFHOOK TONE DIAL ... ;
```

shared dictionary (PROM)

Each task runs a single, high-level, re-entrant definition, of which a simplified version is:

```
: PHONE ( -- )   BEGIN  OFFHOOK  TONE  DIAL
    -BUSY  IF  CONNECT
       ELSE  BUSY  THEN
  AGAIN ;
```

Each task contains private user variables that control its status and action; for example, one cell is 0 if the line is not in use, or points to the line to which it is connected if it is busy.

By letting each task perform its functions sequentially, message passing was virtually eliminated and the only intertask communication was the act of establishing a connection if the called line was available. Even though there were many more tasks, overall performance improved dramatically and the project was a success.

Section 11: Style Recommendations

This section presents two alternate sets of style guidelines plus some suggestions for using symbols in names meaningfully. You may use them as a starting point in developing a style for yourself. If you work in a programming team, we strongly recommend that the team agrees on a set of guidelines and all members follow them. This will make it much easier to share code among yourselves and to maintain it over time.

11.1 FORTH, Inc. Editing Standards

The purpose of this section is to describe the standards used at FORTH, Inc. for editing Forth source code to ensure readability and notational consistency across all Forth systems.

11.1.1 Stack Effects

1. All colon or code definitions must include a comment identifying stack parameters on entry and exit. If no stack parameters are used, an "empty" stack comment is still required.

2. The format of the comment is: (input -- output)

   ...with the rightmost item in each list representing the top of the stack.

   Example 1: **TYPE** (addr n --)   (input only)

   Example 2: **-FOUND** (-- addr1 addr2 flag)   (output only)

   Example 3: **CODE @** (addr -- n)   (both)

   Example 4: **NO-OP** (--)   (no arguments)

3. The stack arguments comment begins one space after the name of the word. The terminating parenthesis should follow the last character, with one space. Exactly three spaces follow the right parenthesis before the code begins. Remember to leave one space after the opening (.

4. The specific description of the stack item should follow these conventions:

addr	address
b	8-bit byte
char	ASCII character
n	single-length number, usually signed
u	single-length, unsigned number
d	double-length, signed number

ud	double-length, unsigned number
flag	Boolean truth flag (0=false)

Other special situations may be dealt with similarly, if necessary to improve clarity, but use single characters where possible. Remember to describe any special notation in source comments!

5. Where there are several arguments of the same type, and if clarity demands that they be distinguished, use ' (prime) or suffix numerals. For example:

   CODE RSWAP (n addr1 addr2 -- n addr1)

   ...shows that the address returned is the same as the first one input.

11.1.2 General Comments

1. All source files should begin with a comment that succinctly describes the contents of the file. This should be followed by any discussion that applies to the file as a whole, a list of required support features that are not part of ANS Forth, and a list of words in the file that are intended for public use (i.e., as distinct from words intended for use only within this file as support words).

2. Before each closely related group of definitions should be a block comment describing the group as a whole (e.g., assumptions or rules of usage) and the individual words in the group. A block comment begins with:

   { --

   ...and ends with:

   -- }

3. Comments within definitions (other than stack effects) should be directed to helping the reader understand what the code is doing from an application perspective, or to elucidating a possibly obscure strategy.

   good: **177566** (SEND +2), **177562** (RCV+2)

   redundant: **DUP 0= ABORT" Value is zero"**   \ Aborts if zero

   unhelpful: **TEMP @**   (Fetch content of TEMP)

   In general, discussions of usage should go in "block comments."

4. Comments should begin with a capital letter and be otherwise lower-case, except as standard usage indicates, e.g.,

   (Defining words)

   (DLL interface)

11.1.3 Spacing Within Files

1. Blank lines are valuable. Use them to separate definitions or groups of definitions.

Avoid a dense clump of lines with a lot of blank lines below, unless the clump is a single definition. A blank line inside a definition is usually unhelpful and should be avoided. Try to leave at least one blank line at the end.

2. Definitions should begin in the leftmost column of a line, with the following exceptions:

   a. If the definition is prefaced by a bar (|) to make it headless, the bar should go in the first column, followed by one space, and the definition begins immediately thereafter.

   b. Two or three related variables, constants, or other data items may share a line if there is room for three spaces between them.

   c. Very short colon definitions may share a line if they are closely related, are spaced properly internally and are separated from each other by at least three spaces.

3. The name of a definition must be separated from its defining word by only one space. If it is a constant or other object with a specified value, the value must be separated from the defining word by only one space.

4. Individual instructions in a code definition must be separated by three spaces. Components of each instruction must be separated by only one space. For example:

```
W R ) MOV   0 W ) MOV B   0 )+ 0 )+ CMP B
```

This makes it easy for a person to identify individual instructions.

5. Second and subsequent lines of colon and code definitions must be indented by multiples of three spaces (e.g., 3, 6, 9). Indentation beyond one set of three spaces indicates nested structures.

6. Examples of Forth in documentation should conform to these rules.

11.2 Naming Conventions

In these tables, "name" refers to some word the programmer has chosen to represent a Forth routine.

Prefixes	Meaning	Examples
!name	Store into *name*	!DATA
#name	1. Size or quantity 2. Output numeric operator 3. Buffer *name*	#PIXELS #S #I
'name	1. Address of *name* 2. Address of pointer to *name*	'S 'TYPE
(name)	1. Internal component of *name*, not normally user accessed 2. Run-time procedure of *name* 3. File index	(IF) (FIND) (:) (PEOPLE)

Prefixes	Meaning	Examples
+name	1. Addition 2. Advance 3. Enable 4. More powerful 5. Takes relative input parameters	+LOOP +BUF +CLOCK +DRAW +SAMPLE
*name	1. Multiplication 2. Takes scaled input parameter	*DIGIT *DRAW
-name	1. Subtract, remove 2. Disable 3. Not name (opposite of name) 4. Returns reversed truth flag (1 is false, 0 is true) 5. Pointers, especially in files	−TRAILING −CLOCK −DONE −MATCH −JOB
.name	1. Print item name 2. Print from stack in format name 3. Print following string. May be further prefixed with data type.	.S .R .$." <string>" D. U. U.R
1name	1. First item of a group 2. Integer 1 3. 1 byte size	1SWITCH 1+ 1@
2name	1. Second item of a group 2. Integer 2 3. 2 cell size	2SWITCH 2/ 2@
;name	1. End of something 2. End of something, start of something else	;S ;CODE
<name	1. Less than 2. Open bracket 3. From device name	<SIZE <# <TAPE
<name>	Internal part of a device driver routine called name	<TYPE>
/name	1. Division 2. Unsigned addition, or ramp up 3. "per"	"/DIGIT /LOOP /SIDE
?name	1. Check condition, return true if "yes" 2. Conditional operator 3. Check condition, abort if bad 4. Fetch contents of name and display	?TERMINAL ?DUP ?STACK ?N
>name	1. Towards name 2. Index pointer 3. Exchange, especially bytes	>R >TAPE >IN >< (swap bytes) >MOVE< (move, swapping bytes)
\name	Unsigned subtraction (ramp-down)	\LOOP
@name	Fetch from name	@INDEX

Prefixes	Meaning	Examples
Cname	1-byte character size, integer	C@
Dname	2-cell size, 2's complement integer encoding	D+
Mname	Mixed single and double operator	M*
Tname	3-cell size	T*
Uname	Unsigned encoding	U.
[name]	Executes at compile time	[']

Suffixes	Meaning	Examples
name!	Store into *name*	B!
name"	String follows, delimited by "	ABORT" <xxx>"
name,	Put something into dictionary	C,
name:	Start definition	CASE:
name>	1. Close bracket	#>
	2. Away from *name*	R>
name?	Same as ?name	B?
name@	Fetch from *name*	B@

Note: Where possible, a prefix before a name indicates the type or precision of the value being operated on, whereas a suffix after a name indicates what the value is or where it's kept.